W9-DAI-394

ASCD MEMBER BOOK

Many ASCD members received this book as a
member benefit upon its initial release.

Learn more at: **www.ascd.org/memberbooks**

MAKE TEACHING SUSTAINABLE

SIX SHIFTS THAT TEACHERS WANT AND STUDENTS NEED

PAUL EMERICH FRANCE

ascd

Arlington, Virginia USA

2800 Shirlington Road, Suite 1001 • Arlington, VA 22206 USA
Phone: 800-933-2723 or 703-578-9600 • Fax: 703-575-5400
Website: www.ascd.org • Email: member@ascd.org
Author guidelines: www.ascd.org/write

Penny Reinart, *Deputy Executive Director;* Genny Ostertag, *Managing Director, Book Acquisitions & Editing;* Mary Beth Nielsen, *Director, Book Editing;* Jennifer L. Morgan, *Editor;* Thomas Lytle, *Creative Director;* Donald Ely, *Art Director;* Yassmin Raiszadeh/The Hatcher Group, *Graphic Designer;* Cynthia Stock, *Typesetter;* Kelly Marshall, *Production Manager;* Shajuan Martin, *E-Publishing Specialist*

All web links in this book are correct as of the publication date below but may have become inactive or otherwise modified since that time. If you notice a deactivated or changed link, please email books@ascd.org with the words "Link Update" in the subject line. In your message, please specify the web link, the book title, and the page number on which the link appears.

PAPERBACK ISBN: 978-1-4166-3229-0   ASCD product #123011
PDF EBOOK ISBN: 978-1-4166-3230-6; see Books in Print for other formats.
Quantity discounts are available: email programteam@ascd.org or call 800-933-2723, ext. 5773, or 703-575-5773. For desk copies, go to www.ascd.org/deskcopy.

ASCD Member Book No. FY23-9 (Aug. 2023 P). ASCD Member Books mail to Premium (P), Select (S), and Institutional Plus (I+) members on this schedule: Jan, PSI+; Feb, P; Apr, PSI+; May, P; Jul, PSI+; Aug, P; Sep, PSI+; Nov, PSI+; Dec, P. For current details on membership, see www.ascd.org/membership.

Library of Congress Cataloging-in-Publication Data

Names: France, Paul Emerich, author.
Title: Make teaching sustainable : six shifts that teachers want and students need / Paul Emerich France.
Description: Arlington, Virginia : ASCD, [2023] | Includes bibliographical references and index.
Identifiers: LCCN 2023012829 (print) | LCCN 2023012830 (ebook) | ISBN 9781416632290 (paperback) | ISBN 9781416632306 (pdf)
Subjects: LCSH: Teachers—Workload—United States. | Teachers—Job satisfaction—United States. | Teachers—Job stress—United States.
Classification: LCC LB2844.1.W6 F73 2023 (print) | LCC LB2844.1.W6 (ebook) | DDC 371.14/12—dc23/eng/20230418
LC record available at https://lccn.loc.gov/2023012829
LC ebook record available at https://lccn.loc.gov/2023012830

32 31 30 29 28 27 26 25 24 23   1 2 3 4 5 6 7 8 9 10 11 12

MAKE TEACHING SUSTAINABLE

SIX SHIFTS THAT TEACHERS WANT AND STUDENTS NEED

Introduction:
Education's Climate Crisis

My last school was tucked away in Chicago's Gold Coast, just steps from the shores of Lake Michigan. Each morning as I drove to school, I would watch the sunrise over Lake Michigan, the seemingly eternal horizon breaking at Chicago's impressive skyline. On the way home, I'd follow the same horizon, now softened by an approaching dusk, back to my home on the North Side.

Driving every day down Lake Shore Drive, I gradually began to notice the little details along my route: the pristinely kept parks, early morning rowers taking advantage of small inlets, the many beaches lining the eastern side of our beautiful city, docks protruding far out into the lake, the lines of wooden posts intended to block boats from encroaching upon beachgoers. Things have changed, though, since I started those morning drives. Large sandbags line Lake Shore Drive now. Our beaches have begun to submerge under consistently rising water. The docks that once reached far into the lake are no longer permitted for use. The wooden posts look like small children trying to prove they can stand in the deep end of the pool.

The reason for the rising lake levels in Chicago is likely not a surprise to you: increasing global temperatures and the changing climate have caused higher than average amounts of rain in Chicago. Although Chicago has attempted to control the problem by installing blockades at some beaches and closing others entirely, the challenge is that the problem is not limited to the city itself. Chicago, as a self-contained entity, does not have the power to stop climate change on its own. Chicago is dealing with the effects of a systemic global problem, attempting to implement measures within its locus of control to keep its residents safe and healthy. But long-term sustainable solutions will require collective effort: a camaraderie among cities, provinces, and nations all over the world to quell the rage of rising tides.

Climate crises are ubiquitous in modern times, from a polarized political climate to an uncertain economic climate, no doubt the result of entrenched yet unsustainable ways of living. A climate crisis currently exists in schools, too. Lack of teacher agency, low pay, boxed curriculum that dehumanizes learning, and high-stakes standardized assessments—these are just a few of education's rising tides, worsening every year and causing more teachers to burn out. Some schools might find temporary local solutions to manage the impending floods, but to truly address the problem of sustainability in the world of teaching requires both a collective effort and a systems thinking approach that will help us get to the root of the problem. These endeavors must proceed in concert with local and individual efforts to truly transform education as a system.

Traditional approaches to the practice of teaching and the profession as a whole have been unsustainable for quite some time, but problems are intensifying. According to a Brookings Institute report (Zamarro et al., 2021), teacher attrition began to worsen in 2021, compared with pre-COVID pandemic attrition rates. The authors compared a RAND Corporation survey from early 2021 with prepandemic data from the National Center for Education Statistics. Whereas prepandemic turnover rates had hovered around 16 percent, nearly a quarter of teachers in the RAND survey shared a desire to leave their jobs at the end of the school year. A 2020 educator confidence report (Houghton Mifflin Harcourt & YouGov) showed similar findings, with 35 percent of teachers planning to leave the profession within the next five years, regardless of years of experience.

Teacher burnout and increased attrition are both detrimental to student learning and costly. In one study, 85 percent of teachers reported that work/life imbalance was affecting their ability to teach (Brackett & Cipriano, 2020; Moeller et al., 2018). Hastings and Agrawal (2015) report that a mere 30 percent of educators are "engaged" in their work; they found that 57 percent are "not engaged" and 13 percent are "actively disengaged." That survey explored the correlations between worker engagement and missed workdays (compared with the baseline of "engaged" teachers). The authors conclude that a lack of engagement in teaching results in increased absenteeism to the tune of millions of missed workdays. Teachers cannot physically, mentally, and emotionally sustain their jobs in current conditions—and this situation comes at great cost to schools and school systems already financially strained. Turnover also can lead to significant financial strain on school districts; it costs approximately $20,000 or more to replace a teacher in an urban district (Carver-Thomas & Darling-Hammond, 2017).

Experts anticipated that the 2021–2022 school year could be the year teachers' intentions to resign turned into action, and it would seem they were right. According to a report from the National Education Association and the Bureau of Labor Statistics (Jotkoff, 2022), there are over 560,000 fewer teachers than there were before the pandemic. Even more dire, the ratio of hires to job openings hovered around 50 percent, meaning that many positions were left unfilled (Jotkoff, 2022). HMH's 2021 *Educator Confidence Report* shores up these findings, noting that educator confidence dropped 7 percent from 2020 to 2021, and that 62 percent of teachers felt somewhat negative (47 percent) or very negative (15 percent) about teaching (HMH & YouGov, 2021).

Beware of those who try to diminish these statistics, suggesting that teachers are not leaving at alarming rates and that the media narrative is misrepresenting the problems schools face (Thompson, 2022). These claims are merely a distraction, further muffling teachers' voices and reinforcing a culture of gaslighting that makes teachers feel undervalued, unseen, and unheard. It is true that teacher retention problems predated the pandemic, however. In her book *Why Great Teachers Quit,* Katy Farber (2010) cites the pressures of standardized testing; ever-increasing expectations; lack of respect; inadequate compensation; and pressures from parents, administrators, and school boards as major contributors to talented teachers leaving the profession.

I am one of the many teachers who chose to take a break from traditional teaching in 2020. I had experienced unsustainable working conditions for years, but my school's response to the pandemic was the proverbial straw that broke the camel's back. I remain connected to learners through a private teaching practice, instructional coaching, and education consulting. With my newfound professional flexibility, I decided to dig deeper into what might be making the teaching profession unsustainable.

The #SustainableTeaching Project

The #SustainableTeaching Project started simply as an idea for a book. I had noticed teachers making pedagogical decisions that were creating unnecessary work for themselves and leading to learning experiences that lacked depth. This unearthed an enduring understanding we will explore together in this book: *Sustainable teaching is good for both students and teachers*. The goal of sustainable teaching is not simply to have teachers do less work; it is to help teachers focus their efforts on effective, efficient, and meaningful practices that make learning richer for students. This aspiration bears some resemblance to the current push to "accelerate learning" in schools, although I urge caution when using that term, as it connotes an increase in the speed at which students learn. Educators should be less concerned about the speed at which children learn and instead direct their efforts toward creating meaningful learning experiences that stick.

As I began writing, I realized that it seemed misguided to center myself as *the* expert on sustainable teaching; after all, sustainability looks different for everyone. This realization revealed another enduring understanding: *Each teacher's pathway to sustainability varies*. Sustainability is inherently a personal topic, contextualized and influenced by varying situations, working preferences, and constraints. We must concurrently cultivate self-awareness in teachers by prompting self-reflection on practices and habits that are unsustainable while also identifying tools, strategies, and practices for shifting toward sustainability.

I subsequently sought more voices for the project. I created and shared the #SustainableTeaching survey on Twitter and Instagram throughout June and July of 2021, with the intention of reaching as many educators and administrators as I could. I began by framing sustainability in terms of three layers: cultural (how educators think about sustainable teaching and learning), pedagogical (what educators do to cultivate sustainable learning experiences), and resource (what educators use to build sustainable learning experiences). After framing sustainability through these three layers, I posed four prompts in separate fields:

- Describe the conditions, practices, or resources you believe to be unsustainable.
- Why do you find these unsustainable?
- Describe the conditions, practices, or resources you believe to be sustainable.
- Why do you find these sustainable?

The questions were intentionally open-ended: I wanted to find out what was most important to each participant without too much prompting or leading.

In the end, I gathered hundreds of survey responses from participants in all 50 states, representing teachers at all levels of education as well as administrators, special education teachers, specials area teachers, and counselors.

I also asked if participants were willing to be interviewed over Google Meet. I did not choose participants randomly for interviews. Instead, I sent emails offering interviews to every participant who expressed interest in being interviewed through early August 2021. These solicitations resulted in more than 70 interviews, totaling over 40 hours. My interview process was consistent each time: I reviewed each participant's survey responses with them and asked them to share more. I made it clear that there were no "right" and "wrong" answers, and that my probing was intended to understand their lived experiences. "If you feel pulled down any one road," I would say, "just run down it. I want to hear what you *really* think."

And they ran down the roads! Although many interviewees recounted issues related to a lack of resources or time, others shared experiences of disrespect, maltreatment, and, in some cases, abuse. Despite these sad and sometimes frustrating stories, their passion for the profession came through. Talking with teachers all over the country reified my own passion for teaching and instilled within me a hope that amplifying this conversation around sustainability could engender substantive change.

Six Mindset Shifts for Sustainable Teaching and Learning

The combination of survey data, interviews, and my own research and reflection on sustainable teaching resulted in the identification of six mindset shifts to change the way educators, coaches, and administrators *think* about teaching. These shifts, accompanied by deeper questions to encourage substantive exploration of the issues, appear below:

- *Humanity over industry.* What is the effect of industrialization on pedagogy? How might we humanize teaching—through identity work and culturally sustaining pedagogy—to create validating and pluralistic classrooms?
- *Collectivism over individualism.* Is an emphasis on individualism sustainable? How might centering collectivist practices build an interdependent classroom culture grounded in authentic care for learning?

- *Empowerment over control.* How effective are compliance-driven practices in the long run? How might we leverage learner and teacher agency, cooperatively building agentive and innovative knowledge acquisition for lifelong learning?
- *Minimalism over maximalism.* How can teachers reduce unnecessary planning and preparation and create rich learning experiences that are embodied and intentional?
- *Process over product.* How might we redefine assessment practices? What might be the benefits of moving from product-oriented measures grounded in acceleration to process-driven assessment that decelerates learning and promotes competence?
- *Flexibility over fixedness.* What are the structures that support responsive teaching, ensuring equitable learning experiences emerge from a constant exchange between teachers and learners?

It is important to note that these mindset shifts are not just for *teachers.* In shifting toward sustainability in our schools, coaches and administrators should identify the conditions, systems, and policies that lie within their locus of control and take steps to improve them. In each chapter, I offer ideas for professional learning written with coaches and administrators in mind.

Six Themes for Sustainable Teaching and Learning

Shifting thinking is not enough—although it can be a great place to start. Change is not linear, and sustainable teaching is not a destination or an achievement. Instead, it is a journey. Along with the six mindset shifts that serve as guiding principles for sustainable teaching, I identified six cross-cutting themes and articulated how the mindset shifts intersect.

The first three themes—healing, regeneration, and vulnerability—ground efforts for sustainability in humanizing teaching and learning. In today's education system, it is all too easy to forget that human beings are the recipients of the standards, assessments, and instructional materials sent their way. Keeping healing, regeneration, and vulnerability front of mind reminds us that we teach *humans,* not content.

The latter three themes—partnership, ritual, and simplicity—lighten teachers' workloads. Teachers are not looking to do less because they are lazy.

They are looking to cut out the practices and resources that do not serve students, while amplifying best practices that *do* support learners. Teachers *want* these practices because they are sustainable—and students *need* them.

Healing

In modern times, educators have a moral imperative to center healing in schools. A focus on healing was likely beneficial for students before the COVID-19 pandemic, but in the past few years, every student in every class in your school has been affected in some way by the global trauma. The response to this trauma is not to go back to the way things were before—working at unsustainable rates, embracing dehumanizing success metrics, and abusing educators who are guiding students through the healing process. Instead, we must ensure classrooms are spaces for collective healing. Students and teachers who come to school pursuing a journey toward wholeness and healing are available to be partners in learning that sticks and sustains—and that partnership is essential for classrooms to be sustainable.

Regeneration

Healing and regeneration go hand in hand. After all, it is hard to heal if you do not give yourself time to regenerate. Just as Earth has an energy budget, humans do, too. For the energy budget to be in balance, the inputs and outputs for energy must remain in sync. The climate crisis is a result of Earth's energy budget being out of balance: we are generating more energy on Earth than can escape Earth's atmosphere, resulting in the emerging effects of climate change like rising sea levels, extreme weather events, and increasing temperatures.

Energy is defined as the ability to do work. Teachers must have a variety of energy sources from which to draw. It is our collective cognitive, emotional, physical, and spiritual energy that sustains teaching in our schools. For teaching and learning to be regenerative, we must allow ourselves time to recharge our batteries. This means sharing in the cognitive, emotional, physical, and spiritual demands of learning with students.

For teachers' energy budgets to be in balance, energy inputs and outputs must also remain in sync. This is not as simple as measuring the number of watts in versus the number of watts out; for teachers, it is much more personal—and personally variable. We need to *believe* teachers when they tell us their energy levels are low or that they are burning out.

Vulnerability

Embracing vulnerability will entail letting go of the urge to control and predict learning in the classroom. Although teachers should make informed pedagogical decisions and consider their effect on students, they do not need to control every moment of an instructional block. Teachers can only control so much. Pursuing sustainability requires acknowledging this truth.

Consider how much of the cognitive, emotional, physical, and spiritual load teachers hold for students. When teachers make the choice to be vulnerable, they share responsibility for these demands with students—which in turn means they no longer have full control over what will emerge in the classroom. This is where it can get scary: to work toward sustainability, you will have to let some things go. You will no longer be able to control or predict events the way you used to. Understand that letting go and opening yourself up to uncertainty is a form of sharing responsibility and, by proxy, building strong partnerships with learners.

Partnership

I tend to think of classrooms as ecosystems. In the natural world, the primary producers of energy are diverse and plentiful: plants are responsible for harnessing and converting the Sun's energy into usable energy for consumers. In too many traditional classrooms, however, it is up to teachers to be the primary producers of learning. Partnering with learners means actively resisting this notion. Instead, *students* become the primary producers of learning. Teachers harvest that energy in the form of evidence of student learning, curating students' conversations, questions, and responses to learning tasks into a sustainable energy source that keeps students learning all year long. This sustainability cannot happen without teacher–student partnership.

Partnering with students and harvesting the fruits of their learning garners myriad benefits. Teachers learn more about students as the students' actions and words contribute to what is known about who they are and how they best learn. Guiding students through the learning process helps them cultivate enhanced self-awareness of their own learning preferences and optimal learning conditions. Teachers can also share the energy demands of learning with students so that teachers are not weathering the demands of learning on their own. Partnership might allow teachers to do less, but that does not mean that less learning is happening in the classroom. Instead, the energy is distributed differently, at times generating even more energy for learning because more human beings are contributing to the learning experience.

Ritual ⧗

Linda Darwich and Alisun Thompson (2021), teacher educators at Lewis & Clark College in Portland, Oregon, identify three Rs for sustainability: relationships, reason, and ritual. They note that "rituals can give us a sense of reliability, peace, and calm" (para. 19).

Although Darwich and Thompson mainly focus on rituals for self-care (e.g., daily walks for reflection and regeneration), self-care alone is not enough to make teaching sustainable. Rituals can be introduced for many reasons. Consider the benefits of having well-practiced yet flexible learning rituals in classrooms. First, the more frequently a ritual is performed, the less cognitive demand it requires: its performance becomes like muscle memory, rather than requiring strenuous thought and effort. Second, a ritual provides a sense of psychological safety and competency. "Oh, we've done this before," students will think. This familiarity makes it easier for them to engage and re-enter the ritual, because they are more likely to feel successful carrying it out. Rituals also allow for learner agency, as students can perform learning rituals independently once they've learned how, adapting them as their needs change.

Rituals should not be mindless. They should support learner agency so that students can share in the energy demands of sustaining learning in the classroom. Rituals should also be flexible enough that they can shift with various tasks while incorporating novelty to make sure students are thinking critically. Teachers need to support students in reflecting on rituals, helping them understand how they can use them on their own or adapt them to meet their needs.

Simplicity ⊘

Simplifying teaching is no easy task. If teaching is oversimplified, it can become reductive, one-size-fits-all, and perhaps even industrialized. To leverage simplicity as a theme for sustainability, its purpose must be to create space and depth in one's teaching practice. Simplifying requires mindfulness and intentionality. It necessitates self-reflection around which practices are serving neither teachers nor students and taking courageous steps to eliminate those practices. This simplification enables amplifying high-impact practices that benefit everyone in the classroom, teachers and learners alike.

Identifying busywork is a powerful prompt for simplification. Are there moments in your school day where students are simply engaged in compliance tasks? Do these tasks help you know and serve learners? Are there assignments you provide or activities you create that fill time or attempt to keep kids busy? Not only is it a disservice to students to have them work for the sake of working, but this practice creates busywork for teachers. *Busywork for students ultimately becomes busywork for teachers.*

How to Use This Book

The path toward sustainability must be action oriented. It is imperative that your study of this book—whether on your own or with a group of trusted colleagues—fosters acts of collective healing and professional growth. If your conversations around sustainability turn into actionless cycles of self-victimization and complaining, they will be counterproductive, chipping away at hope and contributing to further unsustainability of teaching and learning in your school. Instead, acknowledge and validate the very real negative feelings you may have—and then do something with them.

Co-Create a Set of Discussion Agreements

To use this book as a basis for professional development, it is important that everyone participates authentically in discussions of its themes and ideas. Discussion agreements help set and manage expectations, ensuring that discussions are action-oriented and healing. The following examples offer a place to start; feel free to add your own:

- I will speak from the "I" perspective, sharing my lived experiences.
- I will encourage others to speak their truth.
- I will protect the confidentiality of my colleagues. What happens in this discussion stays in this discussion.
- I will respect the agenda, roles, and responsibilities of the group.
- I will validate my colleagues' full range of human emotions.
- I will express my emotions in a reasoned and respectful manner.
- I will use this as a forum for action by identifying clear, concrete action steps after each discussion.
- I will hold myself and others accountable to abiding by these agreements, providing private feedback to colleagues when the agreements are violated.

Start Every Book Discussion with an Agenda

Your discussion agenda should have a clear, tangible goal and should be structured for equity of voice. Consider starting with an open discussion of reactions to the chapter, allowing each person two to three minutes to share their feelings or reactions without interruption. Next, move to an open discussion, either as a whole group or in partners, encouraging participants to dig deeper into ideas or insights raised. Conclude the discussion by identifying concrete action steps that participants can report on at the next gathering. You might want to use the amplify–alter–activate routine as a prompt:

- **Amplify:** Which sustainable practices are you already implementing that you want to keep or increase?
- **Alter:** What do you want to change or stop entirely?
- **Activate:** Which new practices would you like to implement to work toward sustainability?

Assign Roles and Responsibilities

Assign one person to be a timekeeper and another to be a facilitator, keeping the book discussion on track. This may feel a bit strange at first, but remember that structure is healing, especially when discussing heavy topics like abuse or workplace traumas. Providing structure will give participants an idea of what to expect; it will also ensure that no one person dominates the conversation. Switch roles at each book discussion so everyone has a chance to facilitate and keep time.

Take It Slowly

This book is not intended to be read in a few short days, even if it feels like a quick read for you. If you are beginning your sustainability journey on your own, it is best to proceed slowly, creating a reading and reflection calendar for yourself. Each chapter includes reflection prompts to get you thinking about the current reality of your practice, regardless of whether you are working with adult or child learners. Taking time with this process will give you the opportunity to reflect and mindfully evaluate each question within the context of ongoing lived experiences in classrooms and schools. You will not solve the problem of sustainability overnight; the more sustainable approach is to go slowly, allow for lots of quiet moments, and mindfully decelerate your learning so you can soak it in.

Incremental Shifts Toward Sustainability

The path to sustainability must itself be sustainable. You will not solve every problem related to sustainability simply by reading this book and implementing the recommended practices. Some issues and challenges will be outside your locus of control, and others will be unique to your school. The ultimate goal of this book is to provide a thought exercise to help you identify unsustainable practices in your environment.

Consider categorizing the sustainability challenges you identify by the different types of action they require. Some challenges you can act on in your classroom tomorrow. Other challenges will require long-term strategies, and still others will be best addressed in partnership with an administrator, coach, or instructional leadership team.

Keep in mind over the course of this journey toward sustainability that the goal is always *incremental* shifts in practice to gradually create more sustainable behaviors and habits. The true test of sustainability is whether the impact you make *lasts*. Your efforts will be in vain if these incremental shifts do not lead to lasting change. Some might call these effects "learning that sticks," while others might call them "transfer of learning." The degree to which your teaching sticks, sustains, and affects students' real lives can be a metric through which you measure your success with sustainability.

Chapter Summary

Much like Earth itself, education is experiencing a climate crisis. The situation isn't yet hopeless, but simply telling teachers to take better care of themselves will not solve the problem. Instead, we must change the way we conceptualize and enact sustainable instruction in classrooms. We start our journey in the next chapter by exploring how centering humanity can bring us closer to sustainable teaching.

1

Humanity over Industry

ESSENTIAL QUESTION: What does it mean to be human?

My story as a teacher began in the north suburbs of Chicago, where I spent the first four years of my career teaching in a 4th and 5th grade looping class (I taught the same group of students for two years).

At first, I saw teaching as the most important job in the world and dedicated the entirety of my life to it. I was the teacher who came to school on the weekends, organizing my classroom and redoing my bulletin boards. I stayed past sunset, my bursts of lesson planning creativity causing me to lose track of time. I used reclaimed wood from my parents' basement to build custom shelving for the used books I spent my weekends collecting for my classroom library.

"Just wait," one of my colleagues said to me. "Someday you won't do all that stuff anymore. You won't have the energy."

I laughed it off and continued on my merry way. I couldn't understand why others didn't feel exactly as I did about teaching—why it did not consume their thinking and their lives like it did mine. But then, in Fall 2013, everything changed—I realized that the school I had invested so much of my heart and soul into was not willing to reciprocate.

At the time, Illinois had just legalized marriage equality. My straight colleague, Markus, approached me with excitement, proposing a lesson on the new legislation. I was hesitant, as I was not completely out as a gay man at the time, but ultimately I decided to move forward with it. As you can probably anticipate, the administration was not happy with our decision, even though 90 percent of parents were comfortable with an LGBTQ+ lesson taking place in their child's classroom. A very small—and very conservative—minority won in this situation. It was not that they had the most votes; it was that the system was engineered in a way that provided them the most power.

I realized then that the school I had worked so hard to help sustain was not going to support and sustain me, and this realization was devastating. My principal wrote in my evaluation that year that I "professionally withdrew" from the situation, ignorant of the fact that one has no other choice but to withdraw when they are told their identity is not welcomed.

"Maybe in five or 10 years," both the principal and the superintendent said to me at various points. "We just aren't ready for this yet."

My remaining six months in that district were traumatic. In one instance, my principal voiced her desire in a public email to look through my classroom for any "inappropriate" books (code for books with LGBTQ+ content). Although I had been rated as one of the district's *Excellent* teachers the previous year—a distinction offered to only a handful out of hundreds—that year I was not. In a joint decision by the principals and district-level administrators, using an evaluative practice that violated the rules of our collective bargaining agreement, it was determined that "someone like me" who they deemed had poor judgment could not be an "excellent" teacher.

I resigned just months later, refusing the tenure offered to me because I knew I could not work in a place that did not sustain my identity as an openly LGBTQ+ educator. It is important to note that, since that time, the superintendent has apologized for his role in the situation. My principal, numerous other district administrators, and the local board of education have not. In fact, in response to an email I sent the board in 2020, they stated that the "matter was closed."

My story is not unique. I tell it because many teachers experience discrimination and abuse in schools and cannot tell their stories. But these stories must be told if anything is going to change.

"I fear for my life this year," a teacher in a suburban school in Arizona shared in the #SustainableTeaching survey. "As long as voice and freedom to influence the schools is given to [community members railing against critical race theory], there isn't anything sustainable for me this year." She went on to mention that these community members were advocating for "cameras in classrooms and the teaching of only white-centered lies about history."

Approximately one in five respondents in the #SustainableTeaching survey referenced practices and policies related to culturally subtractive pedagogy or culturally sustaining pedagogy, terms coined by Angela Valenzuela (1999) and Django Paris (2012; Paris & Alim, 2017), respectively. It is important to note that this does not mean that other respondents did not consider culturally sustaining pedagogy a sustainable practice; it simply means they did not mention it.

One science teacher in California described working in an environment "rife with implicit bias and a layer of xenophobia, racism, [and] Islamophobia." A 7th grade English teacher from Texas shared, "It is EXHAUSTING as a woman of color to experience the disappointment, despair, and bitterness that comes with watching the systems of oppression our students, families, and other marginalized colleagues face go unchallenged by those of us [without] power." A 4th grade teacher from Maryland shared that she and her colleagues were discouraged from using learners' home languages in the classroom, despite the fact that doing so is both culturally sustaining and a research-based best practice (Paris, 2012; Walqui & Van Lier, 2010).

At the foundation of schools that sustain students' cultures and identities is respect for the sanctity of an individual's humanity—and this goes for teachers, students, administrators, coaches, and anyone else who sets foot in the school. Holding the humanity of all who enter the school sacred is not only imperative, it provides a path to sustainability.

Brené Brown, a shame and vulnerability scholar, describes human connection as "one of our most renewable resources" (2017, p. 117). It is just that: an energy source (Brown, 2010) that can not only sustain humans in their everyday lives but also sustain learning in our classrooms, ensuring all who enter share in the energy demands of learning. Centering humanity—and, by proxy, making space for identity work in schools—provides this connection. When learners, teachers, administrators, parents, staff, and other community members feel seen, heard, and valued, they can derive strength, sustenance, and healing from the vulnerable and authentic relationships they forge, contributing to the overall sustainability of learning within the school.

> Strong relationships help learners heal, allowing them to be active participants in learning.

It is sad to think that some schools have become so devoid of humanity as to require a conversation about "rehumanizing" our schools. How did we get here?

Industry Is Unsustainable

Around the turn of the 20th century, French artist Jean-Marc Côté created a series of drawings envisioning what the world might be like in the year 2000. His drawings are whimsical and outlandish, oftentimes poignantly exaggerating the realities of our current world. He imagined multiple facets of human life, from inventions to recreation and entertainment. He even predicted what school might look like in the year 2000—and as it turns out, he wasn't that far off. In Côté's *At School* (see Figure 1.1), students sit silently in rows, receptacles affixed to their heads, as the teacher grinds books in a machine to disseminate facts, figures, and knowledge.

Although no modern classroom looks exactly like this, Côté's drawing represents a valuable metaphor for the industrialization of learning in schools. Curriculum and textbooks are, in many ways, ground down into digital sand and disseminated through web-based, adaptive tools that industrialize learning. Educators often produce the same effect without digital tools, breaking learning into disembodied bits and pieces or creating worksheets or workbooks intended for mass consumption and regurgitation. The purpose behind this reductive approach is to pursue the quickest path to the highest test scores through the efficient consumption of learning materials—upholding the testing-industrial complex in the process.

FIGURE 1.1

At School (Jean-Marc Côté)

The testing-industrial complex is both a system and a cycle (Croft et al., 2015; Del Carmen Unda & Lizzárraga-Dueñas, 2021). It is a *system* in the sense that it is a web of interconnected organizations and corporations working together to turn assessment and accountability into a lucrative industry. It is a *cycle* in the sense that the actions of these corporations and organizations have created an oppressive dependency on testing, to the point where many cannot see how schools can function without standardized testing and its cousins: boxed curriculum, test-driven teacher evaluation, and test preparation programs.

Industrialization and dehumanization go hand in hand. Prioritizing industrialization decenters humanity for the purpose of amassing wealth. Ecologically, industrialization means extracting and exploiting natural resources, ultimately contributing to the destruction of the planet. In classrooms, it means exploiting both teachers and students for the purpose of raising test scores, ultimately contributing to the dehumanization of teachers, learners, and learning. The education sector's currency is test scores. For curriculum companies, high scores translate directly into dollars earned. Even property values in school districts with high test scores are higher than those with lower test scores, enhancing their monetary value for families.

These incentives cause many to buy into the system. Because testing is baked into the U.S. education system, the stakes are high. Low test scores create real problems, from limited access to higher education to a reduction in home values, not to mention the mental and emotional toll these metrics can take on learners and families. In essence, the industrialization of learning is one of the primary influences on the current unsustainability of education: it dehumanizes and depletes all of us, making us objects of an enterprise.

Centering Humanity for Culturally Sustaining Environments

The way out of the problems caused by the industrialization of education is to humanize learning, finding entry points to gradually dissolve the grip the testing-industrial complex has on schools. School cultures that center humanity are validating and pluralistic, preserving and enhancing connections among all who enter the school. These relationships require vulnerability and are energizing, providing opportunities for regeneration and healing through authentic connection.

Centering humanity serves as a precursor to other mindset shifts. Seeing learners and teachers as human beings, first and foremost, is required to be able to establish collectivist classroom cultures that create the conditions to empower learners. Centering humanity in the interest of sustainable teaching leads to sustained learning. When educators find ways to make vivid connections between who students are and what they are learning, it is more likely that learning will stick and transfer to other areas of their lives (Ernst-Slavit & Egbert, n.d.; Moll et al., 1992).

 Strong relationships energize learners.

Validation

One of my interviews for the #SustainableTeaching Project was with Maribel (Mari) Gonzalez, STEM integration transformation coach at Technology Access Foundation. We talked about the powers of project-based learning and classroom cultures that promote student agency, which Mari described as combating the "subtractive" nature of American schooling (see Valenzuela, 1999).

When schooling is subtractive, its primary motive is to encourage assimilation into the dominant culture (Valenzuela, 1999). This behavior occurs not only in situations where ethnically and linguistically minoritized and marginalized students are forced to conform with whiteness, but also in instances where learning is defined by how closely learners can replicate or regurgitate information and procedures from their teachers, oftentimes measured by performance on standardized assessments. Subtractive schooling cultivates a culture of shame, sending the implicit message that students who diverge from the dominant culture need to be "fixed" or changed.

On the other hand, culturally sustaining schooling dismantles cultures of shame and establishes cultures that validate students' humanity. Culturally sustaining schools seek to "perpetuate and foster—to sustain—linguistic, literate, and cultural pluralism as a part of the democratic project of schooling" (Paris, 2012, p. 93). The gifts students bring to their classrooms and schools—the results of their lived experiences tied to their identities—become the foundation upon which they can build their education. Recognizing and incorporating these gifts and experiences makes students partners in the responsibility of sustaining learning in the classroom. This is also known as *asset-based learning* (Moll et al., 1992).

Asset-based learning allows students to apply their gifts to topics at hand, as opposed to conforming to a predetermined product of learning. The industrialized classroom seeks to create a uniform product, much like an assembly line would. Humanizing classrooms, however, makes it possible for students' diversity to shine in all its pluralistic abundance, encouraging learners to leverage their gifts to help sustain learning.

Pluralism

When educators center learners' gifts—that is, teach in an asset-based manner—schools naturally become pluralistic. The diversity of students' lived experiences and identities manifest in their contributions to classroom learning.

This pluralism is ultimately sustainable. Students' diverse gifts and assets contribute to classrooms in different ways, allowing students to share in the responsibility of caring for the classroom, solving problems, and contributing ideas and energy that will allow the classroom to run on its own. In many cases, this pluralism facilitates students learning with and from their peers, reframing the teacher's responsibilities in the classroom. Striving for uniformity is ultimately unsustainable because teachers must be responsible for monitoring, controlling, and ensuring uniformity—a monumental task that leads to student disengagement *and* teacher burnout.

The pluralistic classroom is good for both teachers and learners. Teachers are no longer the gatekeepers of knowledge and accountants of learning; instead, they remove the gates, partnering with students to create a learning environment where everyone shares what they can do and who they are. Teachers relinquish some of the control that the testing-industrial complex conditions us to crave, allowing students to share in the responsibility of shaping the curriculum and co-constructing knowledge.

STOP AND REFLECT

- How effectively are your classroom and school centering the humanity of learners?
- How does your school and classroom culture validate learner identities?
- What steps have you taken to embrace pluralism in your classroom and school?

Dismantling Industrialization Through Humanizing Pedagogy

"All of us are teachers because we dream of a bigger, broader future for our students," a 1st grade dual-language immersion teacher from California mentioned in the #SustainableTeaching survey. They continued:

> Without a first practice of equity, inclusion, and humanity, many of our students will be blocked out of such a future. In our society, we like to pretend that being a teacher isn't a powerful role. Besides a student's parents, we are in most cases the biggest influence on how they construct and understand their self-identity.

This is a significant responsibility, one that teachers should not take lightly. Centering humanity is sustainable because of the connections and partnerships learners are able to forge. Understanding their own identity will serve learners far beyond the time they spend in any given classroom. This learning transfers into their real lives, sustaining learning long after they have left the classroom. If you're not sure where to start, consider conducting an identity study and planning with the "who" in mind.

When learners feel known, they can build meaningful partnerships that contribute to the sustainability of learning.

Conduct an Identity Study

Identity studies are more than a series of getting-to-know-you activities. They can be the foundation upon which you build a sustainable classroom culture that is validating and pluralistic—something that will be nearly impossible to do if you don't truly know students in the ways they want to be known. Identity studies have three phases: building understanding, self-exploration, and celebrating.

Building understanding. Start with building an understanding of identity by exploring the terms associated with identity work, which will differ based on your students' ages and developmental levels. Consider what key terms and ideas you want them to know before teaching about identity. This is Stage 1 of the "backward design" process (Wiggins & McTighe, 2005), which we will explore further in Chapter 4.

Think about the topics you plan to cover over the course of the school year. How can you ensure students have the prerequisite knowledge related to identity to engage in meaningful conversations about these topics? With younger students, you can use picture books to build the vocabulary foundational to an understanding of identity. Rich children's literature can be used in older grades, and middle and high school students may already have background knowledge on identity so that a review of identity vocabulary may suffice before digging into self-exploration. I prefer to use the "big eight" categories for building identity vocabulary: age, ability, race, ethnicity, gender, sexual orientation, socioeconomic status, and religion—although students can create additional categories as they assimilate identity words.

Self-exploration. After building understanding of identity with intentional vocabulary instruction, allow your students to explore their own identities. In Stage 2 of backward design, Wiggins and McTighe (2005) encourage teachers to identify performance tasks related to the desired results from Stage 1. My performance tasks for identity work have included identity webs, identity murals (see example in Figure 1.2), and identity booklets. In some years, my students have led whole-school identity assemblies to explore, celebrate, and educate others around issues of identity.

FIGURE 1.2

Identity Mural

Student self-exploration looks different in different settings. In an elementary school classroom, self-exploration might look like using picture books as a basis for a class discussion of the elements of identity. Afterward, students might reflect on how they relate to a book character's elements of identity by either writing in a journal or creating a graphic organizer such as a double bubble map (see Figure 1.3).

Middle and high school students can do a similar activity using more complex texts. Teachers might also consider how identity intersects with the content area. For instance, women, women of color, and LGBTQ+ individuals have been historically marginalized in science, technology, engineering, and mathematics (STEM). An identity study could help those who identify with historically marginalized populations see that others like them have made contributions to STEM fields, which creates a pathway for them to contribute to the class. In history classes, understanding identity paves the way for conversations about bias and perspective taking, allowing students to participate in discussions of current events or even the whitewashing of history. With a better understanding of their identities and the ways identities intersect to create power and privilege, they will be better able to delve into these conversations (Crenshaw, 1989).

Celebrating. Celebrating learning is a sustainable practice within any unit of study (see Chapter 5). Ending units with a learning celebration provides

FIGURE 1.3

Double Bubble Map

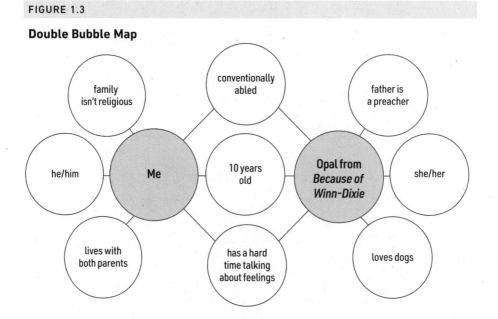

opportunities for recognizing growth, reflecting on challenges, and identifying action steps for future learning. It also contributes to building the humanizing culture needed for sustainable classrooms: students experience affirmation and validation of their successes, connecting their efforts to fruitful learning and creating a sense of mastery. A *sense of mastery*—the ability to connect one's efforts to progress—contributes to sustainability.

Pluralism can also be found in the diversity of learning products in a celebration, providing all learners with more models of what fruitful learning can look like. This is especially true for identity work. By ending identity units with a celebration, learners not only validate their peers' efforts but also learn about the ways in which they are similar to and different from their peers. This lays the groundwork for meaningful learning partnerships where students can be vulnerable, make mistakes, and take risks together.

> A sense of mastery is regenerative, giving students the confidence to contribute to learning without the teacher present.

Plan with the "Who" in Mind

The value of identity work expands beyond building classroom community. Starting the year with identity work allows teachers to plan with the "who" in mind.

It wasn't until recently that I realized Wiggins and McTighe's (2005) work on backward design was, in some ways, incomplete—inspired by a response to a tweet I posted: "The first question you ask when designing curriculum should never be: What are we using? The first question you ask should be: What are we trying to learn?"

A science teacher in Ohio replied: "No mention of the people you are teaching. Gotcha."

Their response helped me see that industrialization was coloring my perspective. It makes no sense to prioritize the content over the human, and perhaps this is where far too many teachers, schools, and districts go wrong. We don't teach content; we teach human beings.

There is no escape from the realities of modern schooling. Educators are held accountable to teaching core literacies, including English, mathematics, the sciences, and humanities. However, there must be a way to strike a balance between teaching to standards and nurturing our students' humanity. There is a way to incorporate both in our instruction—what we hope students will learn and who they are.

Incorporate identity into all you teach. This might sound like a daunting task, but it doesn't have to be. Consider small ways in which you can incorporate lessons on identity into already existing curricula. You might have students start the year reflecting on their identities as readers, writers, scientists, mathematicians, and historians. As the year progresses, you will need to find other ways to come back to identity. Figure 1.4 presents some ideas for incorporating identity in multiple subject areas.

FIGURE 1.4

Incorporating Identity into Core Literacies

Subject	Activities to Incorporate Identity
Reading	Have students create a reading timeline where they share books that have been important to them throughout their lives. They can add to this timeline or make a new one as they read more books over the course of the year. This activity helps students reflect on their identity as a reader over the year and helps teachers better understand students as readers.
Writing	Conduct a genre study in which you choose the genre (based on grade-level standards) to ensure appropriate coverage, but let students choose a topic within the genre so that they can incorporate their interests and topics that are important to them. Offering students choice allows them to incorporate the pieces of themselves they want seen.
Math and science	Create bins of books or libraries of digital resources for students to learn about marginalized mathematicians, engineers, and scientists within the various strands of mathematics and science (e.g., geometry, data science, physics, chemistry, engineering). Choose an individual to focus on in each new unit.
Social studies	Ask students to consider how an individual's identity might influence their actions or ways of thinking. Maps are laden with bias; understanding *who* makes maps can help students understand how maps can be used to perpetuate oppression. Similarly, using an identity lens, students can understand how systems of oppression can influence governments and infiltrate democracies around the world.
Physical education	Athletic culture often centers conventionally abled individuals. Share knowledge about marginalized athletes, highlighting voices from LGBTQ+ and disabled populations in addition to Black and Brown athletes. Consider aligning these athlete spotlights with current events (e.g., major sporting events).
Music and art	Assess the proportion of the curriculum dedicated to artists with dominant identities (i.e., white, straight, cisgender, conventionally abled). Ask students about the types of art and music they enjoy and incorporate studies that align with essential art and music skills. Consider spotlighting marginalized musicians and artists and/or incorporating music from students' home cultures into units of instruction.

Revisit identity work throughout the school year, prompting students to explore how their identities have changed. You might even conduct multiple identity studies, perhaps at the beginning of each unit or semester. Involve learners in documenting their exploration of identity. Mindfully documenting these experiences (e.g., through journals or portfolios) encourages students to reflect on how their identities have evolved throughout the year.

Build rich classroom libraries. A rich classroom library filled with authentic children's literature is one of the most sustainable resources out there. It is both culturally and curricularly sustaining.

One teacher from a suburban school in Texas shared:

> History texts are outdated almost as soon as they are published. We should be learning history from multiple sources, not wasting money on a whitewashed version. The districts should be providing a number of multicultural resources instead, relieving stress and time from teachers to find what they need.

This statement speaks to the importance of curating a rich and diverse classroom library that provides learners with books that reflect their own experiences and creates a validating and culturally sustaining environment. Books can also enable regeneration and healing through reading. Educators can create rituals around their classroom libraries, teaching students how to use them and finding rhythm in adding new titles. This practice supports *all* learners—even those with culturally dominant or privileged characteristics.

"Some of these students haven't met a person of color," a middle school teacher from Vermont shared with me, "or somebody who is not Christian."

Seeing oneself in the curriculum is both validating and healing, incentivizing learners to make contributions to learning.

Books can provide access to others' lived experiences, affecting students' lives beyond the four walls of the classroom. Not taking steps to talk about identity with white students—or students who are Christian, cisgender, straight, or exhibit any other marker of dominant culture—creates schools that are inherently unsafe and culturally subtractive places for students of color, LGBTQ+ students, students with disabilities, and others who feel forced to assimilate. Much like I did, these students will withdraw if they cannot see themselves in the classroom, which limits their ability to contribute to the overall sustainability of learning.

A rich classroom library also includes diverse instructional materials. Learning tasks and texts should create opportunities for students to see themselves in the curriculum, whether by incorporating students' interests, using names that reflect their cultural backgrounds, or referencing situations in which they might find themselves. Industrialized curricula, inherently biased toward dominant culture, will not reach all learners, raising questions about how teachers can adapt existing materials to appeal to all learners. Is there a way to design units of instruction that incorporate learner identity through curating resources that are already on hand?

Oftentimes, these changes are rather simple. When teaching a group of predominantly 3rd grade Black students about area and perimeter, I shared the story of Jasmine Jefferson, founder of Black Girls with Gardens. Afterwards, learners had to calculate the area and perimeter of rectangular garden boxes for one of Miss Jasmine's gardens. This required just a minor modification to the task and resulted in increased engagement and a connection to identity.

Find purpose in the humanity of academics. Many educators ground their instruction in college and career readiness. Although well intended, these lessons rarely resonate with kids—especially the most marginalized and vulnerable learners. Moreover, students will not directly use all the skills identified by state and national standards in college or their careers. After all, the average adult does not need to demonstrate proficiency in "distinguishing their own point of view from the narrator" of a story on a day-to-day basis— but that does not mean there is not deeper meaning in that standard that will transfer to other disciplines or areas of life.

Why *do* we want students to be able to read stories and distinguish their point of view from the narrator? It is because we want them to consider others' perspectives and think critically. The standard isn't just about college or career readiness; it's about building transferable competencies that help them connect with and understand the surrounding world. Teachers need to ground the purpose for learning in the humanity of the skills they are trying to teach students, which is inherently more meaningful—and more sustaining—for learners.

For example, consider presenting to students the concept that mathematics is a language—something that human beings came up with thousands of years ago to keep track of quantities and talk about shapes. I have shown students examples of ancient number systems, from ancient Egyptian to Mayan and Babylonian, a strategy I learned as an undergraduate at the University of Illinois Urbana-Champaign. After presenting such tasks, I provide students time to explore them, deciphering the symbols on their own or even describing the number systems in terms of place value. As an extension, I give them additional numbers to translate, helping learners see math as a language through which one can understand and interact with the world. "Language" expands beyond printed and spoken alphabetic text.

Implications for Professional Learning

Adults cannot teach about identity without first doing the work themselves. This means that if you want to incorporate identity into a culturally sustaining approach to teaching and learning, then you must carve out time for adults to have vulnerable conversations about identity and how it affects the ways we interact with our classroom, curriculum, and learners.

Consider creating a professional learning plan specifically grounded in identity work over the course of the year, similar to the student identity unit plan suggested previously. Figure 1.5 presents a sample of what professional learning goals could look like, month to month.

> Before learners can be vulnerable with their identities, adults must first be vulnerable with theirs.

FIGURE 1.5

Professional Learning Plan for Identity

Month	Learning Goal
September	We will develop a collective definition of *identity*.
October	We will define *group identity* and identify major categories of group identity (i.e., gender, race, ethnicity, socioeconomic status, religion/spirituality, ability, sexuality, age).
November	We will recognize that elements of our identities intersect to form unique individuals (*intersectionality*).
December	We will recognize traits of dominant culture and discuss the effect of dominant culture on minoritized or marginalized cultures.
January	We will cultivate understanding of the power and privilege various identities hold.
February	We will identify how our curricular resources reflect bias and privilege.
March	We will identify ways to adapt our curriculum so that it better represents our student population.
April	We will create interdisciplinary identity units connected to core content to start with our students in the fall.
May	We will reflect on our exploration of identity, setting goals for next school year.

Personalization Requires Seeing the Person

In 2022, I spent some time in Texas working with a school district on personalized learning practices. In preparing for the experience, I spoke with the chief academic officer (CAO), previewing some of the content I planned to share. During our meeting, the CAO asked me to modify the language on my slides, specifically editing out words like "identity."

A week before my visit, a few families from the district caught wind that I would be working with teachers. This created controversy, with parents attending the school board meeting to oppose my visit, in part because of my identity as a queer educator but also because my work incorporated unpacking "learner identity."

"We just want to focus on the *work*," the CAO said to me, implying that the true work of personalization was about reaching learners' academic needs. I stressed that *identity is the work*. How can teachers be expected to meet all learners' needs without talking about who their students are? The CAO was not considering students' full identities—and failing to do so limits avenues to build culturally sustaining classrooms that validate learners and encourage them to share in the demands of fruitful, transferable learning. In Chapter 2, we will build on this enduring understanding about the importance of identity work, examining how it contributes to a collectivist classroom culture where learners share in energy demands of sustaining learning within a community.

Chapter Summary

To be human is to learn, and to learn is to be human. The humanity of learning relies on connection, and these connections provide classrooms with a sustainable energy source. Teachers need to implement culturally sustaining practices that help learners know and connect with each other. These practices also help learners make meaningful connections between themselves and the curriculum and find purpose and relevance in what they are learning. When learners feel seen, heard, and validated, they are more inclined to see themselves in the collective, engage with it, and share in the demands of learning.

STOP AND REFLECT

Identify some action steps you can take to shift toward humanizing learning.

- **Amplify:** Which sustainable practices are you already implementing that you want to keep or increase?
- **Alter:** Which new practices do you want to change or stop entirely?
- **Activate:** What would you like to implement to work toward sustainability?

2

Collectivism over Individualism

ESSENTIAL QUESTION: Where do we derive our energy from?

Many of the responses from the #SustainableTeaching survey shared in Chapter 1 came from places of unsustainability, burnout, or exhaustion. My conversation with Ricky Martin, an instructional coach in North Carolina, was different.

Ricky told me that he drives 100 miles each day between his home and school. My initial reaction was that the commute itself was unsustainable. However, listening to Ricky share his thoughts about his school and school culture, I learned why he chooses to make this daily commute—even though working at a school closer to home would lessen his commute and perhaps even pay more.

> I think the big thing [is] having admins that are willing [to do] what my admin has done for nine years. Filter . . . , stand up . . . , be willing to put themselves on the line for what is best for students and teachers.

Ricky described the ways this administrative buffer manifests in his school, including how the administrative team lessens teacher workload by offering teachers support with compliance paperwork and provides "tap out" release time for teachers when they are overwhelmed or need a break. His school leaders embrace a collectivist mindset, one where all adults share in the collective responsibility of caring for *all* kids. At his school, he said, "they're all our kids." Every student in the school, which has a population of about 400, is "one of our Bears. That's the mascot."

Ricky's principal, Leah Leonard, shared her reflections on what creates a strong school culture: "I have always been the believer of 'If you don't have happy teachers, you will not have happy children.' When I grow teachers, I will in turn grow children. I have always put my emphasis on teachers."

Leah described taking a systems-thinking approach and "getting to the root cause" of problems or challenges, going beyond survey data. Although her school's teacher working conditions surveys had positive scores, she learned that the scores did not reflect the authentic sentiments of her staff. By building strong relationships with her staff and talking with them regularly, she learned there was a lot of work to be done. She is also a firm believer in giving teachers voice, providing authentic support, and building trust, referring to these practices as building an "emotional bank account."

One step Leah took was to include classroom teachers whenever she met with families of students. Her overt support for teachers started building "that 'emotional bank account,'" she said, "so when I had to make a debit from that bank account, I didn't put it on overdraft."

Building relationships does not require relinquishing expectations, structure, or boundaries. Instead, they are built on an *exchange,* a relationship where administrators can make requests of teachers in addition to supporting teachers and meeting their requests. Such relationships contribute to sustainability because they are grounded in partnership and allow all individuals space and time to regenerate.

Administrators who partner with teachers contribute to sustainability by listening to them, advocating for their well-being, and having their backs. As a result, teachers can let their guard down and be vulnerable with challenges.

These reflections scratch the surface of the true meaning of "collectivism." The term originates from the Latin *legere,* meaning "to gather": collectivism is a gathering. In schools, it means leveraging each other's strengths, being vulnerable with your own challenges, and converging around a shared vision for teaching and learning that is humanizing, inclusive, and sustainable.

Individualism Is Unsustainable

How does collectivism mesh with what we explored in Chapter 1? On the surface, identity work seems grounded in individualism. Pursuing identity work and centering students' humanity sends a very clear message that individuals matter in the classroom.

We live in a society that tells stories of rugged individualism—the value of working hard and making good choices—suggesting that one's destiny is determined solely by the amount of work done and the choices made. There is ample evidence to suggest otherwise. In our society, social mobility is much harder for people born into poverty, centuries of systemic racism have produced a measurable Black–white wealth gap, and LGBTQ+ teens are much more likely than their cisgender-heterosexual peers to commit suicide (Johns et al., 2020). All these examples stem from systemic barriers and environments built by a society that marginalizes those with nondominant characteristics.

This individualistic way of thinking has made its way into the classroom, where students are often blamed for perceived deficits. When they struggle, they are told to work harder or pay better attention. In many classrooms, learning is a competition, either through percentile-ranked standardized assessments, leveling, or gamified applications that coax students into compliance through point totals and badges.

These inherently competitive tools are offered as solutions for "personalizing" learning, a concept that has grown in popularity following the COVID-19 pandemic. It has always been true that students enter classrooms coming from different places, having had varied experiences. Must we therefore take an individualized approach to teaching and learning? Instead, consider seeing, hearing, and honoring the individual needs of learners while helping them feel connected to the collective learning environment so they may find camaraderie, community, and belonging. These values lie at the heart of differentiated instruction: differentiating the learning environment promotes access and belonging, as opposed to unsustainably individualizing curriculum.

Within this context, identity work is not individualistic at all—at least not in the competitive, rugged sense. *Identity work in the classroom is inherently collectivist.* Its goal is to acknowledge the humanity in each individual student, paving pathways to belonging within an interdependent network of learners.

This concept has implications beyond classroom culture. Individualistic pedagogies have contributed to the unsustainability of teaching. Misguided approaches to differentiated instruction or personalized learning typically entail using data to create levels of learners, after which teachers or digital algorithms align instructional resources to these levels. On the surface, this tactic appears sensical, but the deficits of this style of differentiation demonstrate that it is unsustainable and inequitable. Grouping students based solely on instructional level limits their opportunities to find value and strengths in all peers. It also exacerbates opportunity gaps; learners with high achievement scores receive access to more rigorous curriculum, while others are restricted to below-grade-level curriculum. The most extreme versions of personalized learning engender social isolationism in addition to widening opportunity gaps, which can create unhealthy competition in the classroom as learners compare themselves with each other based on their levels (France, 2022).

Rather than a competitive hierarchy where learners with high test scores are afforded more privileges, the collectivist classroom is a network of learners, each student a node in the network. Each node offers both gifts and challenges to the classroom. Depending on the day, the task, or the situation, all learners find opportunities to amplify their gifts to support the collective as well as draw from their network when they need support in overcoming a challenge. This concept gets to the heart of the sustainability of collectivism: through partnership, learners step up and step back when appropriate, sharing in the energy demands required to create rich learning experiences in the classroom. Students expend energy when they step up; their energy is regenerated when they step back.

> Learners can regenerate and replenish their energy reserves when they alternate between stepping up and stepping back.

Assessment, instructional resources, and pedagogy are still relevant to a conversation about collectivism. The focus of the collectivist classroom culture—a culture of *we* instead of a culture of *me*—supports practices that help students and teachers reach their instructional goals.

Centering Collectivism for a Humanizing Culture

"Sustainable conditions and overall well-being are a part of regenerative practice," shared Lisa Julian Keniry, founder of Green Teach for Opportunity, in the #SustainableTeaching survey. "Sustainability is about healing the soul and the planet. . . . If conditions for teachers are not sustainable, this reflects a broader crisis of Earth and mind."

Lisa's reflection reveals two keys that can unlock pathways to sustainability. Embracing a collectivist mindset provides opportunities to regenerate and heal together from both the trauma and challenges presented by the COVID-19 pandemic and the preceding decades of systemic teacher abuse and oppression. Everyone—teachers, coaches, and administrators alike—benefits from a culture that promotes a collective responsibility to serve all students in the school. There is strength in mutualism. Every person on the team rests easy knowing that someone has their back, that they can step back when they need to regenerate, and that they can find healing and belonging through community. This strength can be achieved through interdependent school cultures grounded in authentic care for learning.

To heal from decades of educational trauma requires making space for regeneration and a sense of belonging in schools.

Interdependence

In *Culturally Responsive Teaching and the Brain,* Zaretta Hammond (2015) differentiates between independent and dependent learners, noting that *independent learners* do the following:

- Rely on the teacher to carry some of the cognitive load temporarily
- Utilize strategies and processes for tackling a new task
- Regularly attempt new tasks without scaffolds
- Have cognitive strategies for getting unstuck
- Have learned how to retrieve information from long-term memory (p. 14)

These qualities align with the qualities of sustainable teaching: through partnership, learners share the energy demands of learning by making choices for themselves. Let's build on Hammond's definition of an independent learner to characterize *interdependent learners* in the classroom as students who do the following:

- Rely on teachers and peers to carry some of the load temporarily
- Support other learners by carrying the cognitive load temporarily
- Possess a conscious knowledge of self so that they can lend their strengths to others and know when to seek help
- Articulate the gifts their peers bring into the classroom, seeing each peer as a valuable partner in learning, regardless of academic level or test scores

- Leverage their network of peers to engage with, contribute to, and find belonging within the collective consciousness of the classroom

Educators are trained to think of the classroom in terms of hierarchical structures rather than as a network. This is evident in traditional classrooms that center the teacher as the gatekeeper and disseminator of knowledge. Teachers inadvertently reinforce the testing-industrial complex when they label and group learners by standardized test scores. Most adults today, including teachers and parents of school-age children, grew up in the era of standardized testing, so it can be a struggle to envision a different reality for themselves and today's learners.

What if educators thought of classrooms as networks instead of distinct groups of high-achieving, on-level, and low-achieving learners? What might it look like to see each child as a node within a network, each of whom possesses strengths and challenges not simply related to academics? This mindset shift would have major implications on building curriculum, assessing learners, and delivering instruction. Conceiving of the classroom as an interdependent network of learners aids in centering this essential idea: for classrooms and instruction to be sustainable, hierarchies and competitive learning cultures must be dismantled and replaced by the idea that caring for and being accountable to others is just as important as caring for and being accountable to oneself.

Caring

School is often centered around the concept of work. This comes as no surprise; our society was built upon the extraction and exploitation of natural resources, the industrialization of these commodities, and the subjugation of minoritized and marginalized individuals for the purpose of amassing wealth and privilege, resulting in the environmental and cultural crises we see today. American society, contextualized by a free-market economy and influenced by an emphasis on rugged individualism, has convinced us that the path to success and fulfillment is work—that if we work hard enough, our hard work will liberate us, allowing us to achieve the American dream. Ultimately, we are conditioned to tolerate the abuse of the American culture of *work*.

This abusive culture of work is unsustainable. It burns us out and siphons precious time and energy from the very things that make us human—our friends, families, and interests—all because we believe we can achieve the American dream. The reality is that the type of social mobility enshrined in the American dream requires a degree of wealth and privilege—or just plain luck—and thus is afforded only to some. It is a story that incentivizes an unsustainable industrialized mindset, and those who believe the story write their own narrative in its image.

But working harder and harder in schools is not helping anyone achieve any sort of American dream: it's just burning teachers out and chipping away at students' love of learning. Instead of classrooms being places that require working harder and doing more, they should be settings in which all learners feel empowered to help sustain learning. Learning as a collective effort starts with creating cultures of genuine caring in schools. Valenzuela (1999) notes:

> When the cared-for individual responds by demonstrating a willingness to reveal her/his essential self, the reciprocal relation is complete. . . . Even well-intentioned students and teachers frequently find themselves in conflict. At issue, often, is a mutual misunderstanding of what it means to "care about" school. (pp. 21–22)

Valenzuela differentiates between aesthetic care and authentic care. *Aesthetic care* aligns more closely with the industrialized culture of work. When students "care" about school aesthetically, their care is grounded in compliance metrics—turning in assignments on time, behaving within the confines of the dominant culture, doing what the teacher says. These behaviors are unsustainable; they not only require a great deal of effort on the part of both teachers and students to manage compliance metrics but also counteract any intrinsic motivation to participate in learning. Instead of students being partners in a genuine care for learning and school, teachers end up defining, managing, and doing the "caring" on their behalf.

"Relational teaching encourages us to build relationships with our students because they're humans in our circle who need care and that we care about," shared one middle and high school instructional coach from Michigan. They continued:

> These relationships are too often weaponized to get our students to be compliant and more easily controlled, but sustainable relationships rooted in relational teaching don't have this end. In other words, "caring for" is sustainable, while "caring about" is less so.

When learners and teachers share in the responsibility of caring, it becomes a renewable resource that powers classrooms. For cultures of care to be sustainable, everyone must participate and share in the responsibility of building a classroom culture grounded in authentic care: caring about learning, caring about oneself, caring about others. The time to establish this kind of culture cannot be mindlessly accelerated for the purpose of finding the most efficient route to the highest test scores.

STOP AND REFLECT

Identify some action steps you can take to shift toward humanizing learning.

- How effectively are your classroom and school building a collectivist learning culture?
- In what ways are your classroom and school interdependent?
- In what ways are those in your school instilling a culture of authentic care for learning?

Teaching to Honor the Collective

Shifting toward collectivism does not mean going back to a one-size-fits-all curriculum, nor does it require ignoring individual learning needs. It simply means that learners know and understand that their individuality is equally as important as the health and well-being of their peers and the classroom community. This comprehension requires intentionally building classroom culture around collectivism and dismantling hierarchies in classrooms so that learners are not in competition with each other.

Ultimately, the goal of collectivist pedagogy is that all learners feel seen, heard, and valued so that they can contribute to the collective learning community as a valuable node in their learning network. Achieving this goal requires teaching with vulnerability, partnering with students, and giving up some control. It might also entail retiring some of the long-held ideas of what school is supposed to look like. Fear not. This does not mean letting go of everything all at once; it means mindfully choosing to make incremental shifts in teaching toward collectivism.

For teaching to become sustainable, teachers must open themselves up to uncertainty and give more control to learners.

Intentionally Build Classroom Culture

Building a collectivist classroom culture requires more than simply telling learners to care for themselves, others, and their learning: students need to be taught how. Building classroom culture can easily coincide with the identity studies discussed in Chapter 1. Your classroom should have an emerging identity as a result of conversations around classroom agreements, roles and responsibilities, team building, and how to manage ongoing class meetings where learners celebrate collective successes and navigate challenges as a group. Intentionally building classroom culture ensures that teachers and learners alike are stewards of learning in the classroom, with all class members sharing the responsibilities of sustaining learning.

  When teachers trust learners with caring for learning in the classroom, their jobs become simpler because there is less to do.

Set agreements, roles, and responsibilities. In *The First Six Weeks of School*, Responsive Classroom (2015) offers a structure for setting up classroom agreements. First, learners generate ideas for what classroom agreements should look like. Then, the teacher facilitates a discussion where learners collectively synthesize these rules into three overarching agreements that encompass all other rules. One of my classes came up with the overarching rule "Be your best self." We applied this rule to a variety of contexts, from interpersonal conflicts to intentionality around classroom tasks. This activity builds a genuine culture of caring because students' voices directly contribute to creating classroom agreements. Learners are more likely to care about classroom elements to which they have contributed.

Many teachers already collectively generate classroom agreements. This activity can serve as a powerful assessment, offering insight into how learners see themselves, their peers, and their teacher. It also provides you with the opportunity to reframe learners' perceptions about their roles in the classroom, especially if their perceptions of school are grounded in industrialized, compliance-based models.

To reframe learners' perceptions and lay the foundation for a collectivist classroom culture, put learners into groups and pose a few questions:

- In this classroom, what should I hear the teacher saying? What should I see the teacher doing?
- In this classroom, what should I hear students saying? What should I see students doing?

Ask the groups to share their responses with the whole class, then lead a class discussion comparing and contrasting their ideas—and adding your own. Students often respond along the lines of teachers "helping students," "giving out work," "collecting assignments," and "showing us how to do things," and students "waiting their turn to talk," "completing their work," and "doing what the teacher says." For students to care for learning in the classroom, however, slightly different roles and responsibilities on the parts of both teacher and learner are required (see Figure 2.1).

Share the chart in Figure 2.1 with students and discuss how these responsibilities differ from their first responses. Ask if their thinking has changed. Students can also reflect individually on the activity by completing a journal entry about the discussion and activity. Reconvene the groups for further discussion, then have the whole class work together to synthesize their final ideas into a single list of class roles and responsibilities. Revisit these responsibilities throughout the year, perhaps in morning meetings once a month or as you and your students identify new responsibilities.

Take time for team building. If you want your students to operate as a team, you must teach them how. In my practice, this has included team-building games at the start of the year. One of my favorites is Classroom Crossword.

On the first day of school, as students enter the classroom, they create their name using die-cut letters on square pieces of paper. For the activity, I ask students to collectively create a crossword for the bulletin board incorporating everyone's name (see Figure 2.2). "Because we want to have a classroom where everyone is included," I say, "it's important that *everyone's* name makes it in."

This activity can be a bit chaotic—which is OK. An activity like this, which may be new to your students, provides an authentic assessment of how your

FIGURE 2.1

Roles and Responsibilities in Building Classroom Culture

Teachers	Students
• Ask questions • Meet with small groups • Meet with individuals • Find tasks for the class to collaborate on • Review learning artifacts • Help keep portfolios organized • Celebrate learners' strengths and identify challenges • Give and receive feedback	• Ask questions • Make choices that help me learn • Talk to friends or peers about learning • Find something to do if I finish early • Think: "What tools do I have to solve this problem on my own?" • Make independent attempts before asking someone for help • Give and receive feedback

Classroom Crossword

learners collaborate, showing you who tends to step forward and direct others and which students need support or coaching with getting involved.

If you notice your class needs more directed coaching to complete the task, offer them that support. What is most important is reflecting on the activity after it has concluded. Ask students to identify strategies and behaviors that made it easier (or harder) to accomplish the task. What worked? What didn't work? I begin by asking learners to turn and talk to a partner about what did and did not work, collecting their responses on a T-chart the class can continue to refer to during future team-building activities.

 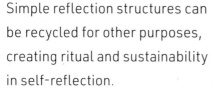
Simple reflection structures can be recycled for other purposes, creating ritual and sustainability in self-reflection.

The what-worked-and-what-didn't list should be a living and breathing document. As your class engages in more team-building activities (see suggestions in Figure 2.3) or independent, small-group, or other work, direct students to reflect on their efforts in the context of the list, adding to or revising it throughout the year. You might consider setting classwide goals related to the list, particularly if your students need to build their skills mitigating conflicts, ensuring equity of voice, or inviting classmates to participate. Keeping your finger on the pulse of competency in teamwork will both

FIGURE 2.3

Team-Building Activities

Invisible Path	Create a grid on the floor. The larger the grid, the more rigorous the task. On the grid will be an invisible path only you know about. Learners have to find the invisible path through trial and error. Once a student selects an incorrect square, they have to try again. This activity teaches students to learn from others' mistakes.

		X		
	X	X		
	X			
	X	X	X	X
				X

Spider Web	Using yarn or string, create a web with three to five openings in the entryway to your classroom. The object of the game is for the entire class to pass from one side of the web to the other without touching the web. In some cases, this might require using a chair or even lifting participants up. When the entire class is through, they have won the game! This activity teaches learners to think strategically and work together.

DOOR

Classroom Connections	Have students sit in a circle. Holding on to one end of a ball of yarn, toss the ball to someone else in the circle while offering the recipient a compliment or affirmation. As the yarn travels to each member of the circle it creates a web: a concrete representation of how everyone is connected. Ask specific learners to let go of the string to demonstrate what happens when someone "lets go" of their responsibility to participate in and support the class. The result: the web falls apart. This activity teaches students the importance of their individual contributions to the collective group.

instill a collectivist mindset and empower learners to make choices that contribute to the overall sustainability of your classroom.

Nurture classroom culture with class meetings. A collectivist classroom culture requires regular class meetings (see Figure 2.4 for a list of meeting types). Class meetings create a ritual for addressing classroom issues or reflecting on successes, challenges, and next steps for teamwork. They also provide an opportunity for lessons on social skills, emotional intelligence, or executive function skills (see Chapter 3).

 Creating rituals around class meetings and reflection on teamwork sets an expectation that all members will work together to sustain learning in the classroom.

Dismantle Competition

A shift toward collectivism will affect the way you think about curriculum, assessment, and instruction. Many assessment practices are grounded in a competitive mindset—no doubt an extension of an American economic system that rests on the idea that competition supports innovation. It might be true that healthy competition is part of a capitalist economy, but classrooms are not miniature capitalist economies. As one elementary special education teacher

FIGURE 2.4

Ideas for Class Meetings

Type	Description
Morning meeting	At the beginning of the school day, convene all learners together. Responsive Classroom (2016) suggests including a greeting, time for sharing, a group activity, and a morning message.
Closing meeting	Use one of the following structures to reflect on how the day has gone: • **Two Stars and a Wish.** What were two things that went well today? What do you hope goes differently tomorrow? • **Rose-Bud-Thorn.** What went well today (rose)? What are you excited about (bud)? What didn't go well today (thorn)?
Problem and solution	When a problem or challenge arises in the classroom, gather students and ask them to generate ideas for solutions. Have learners write their ideas on sticky notes, and group the notes by theme. Decide as a class which solution(s) to try.
Shout-outs	Offer an opportunity for students to praise their peers with a "shout-out." You will need to coach students on how to be specific with their compliments, describing what their peer did or said and what the effect was.
Intentions and goal setting	Set weekly goals or intentions as a class, and hold a class meeting at the end of the week to reflect qualitatively on successes and challenges. This activity creates accountability and gives learners agency with generating ideas for next steps.

shared in response to the #SustainableTeaching survey, "A school culture that is built on competition . . . is unsustainable."

Consider the following dos and don'ts for dismantling competition in favor of collectivism.

DON'T level learners publicly. Although assigning learners to leveled groups might help teachers efficiently deliver curriculum aligned with identified levels, sustainable differentiation encompasses more than efficiency. Leveling learners publicly—whether through groups, self-pacing charts, or behavior clip charts—stigmatizes students. It is an inequitable, harmful, and unsustainable practice that depletes energy in the classroom and frames learners in terms of their deficits, ultimately subtracting from their identities. In response, learners who already feel marginalized and need support will be even less likely to engage with the collective and offer their gifts to the classroom.

DO use criterion-referenced assessment to inform approaches and next steps for learners. *Criterion-referenced assessment* refers to standardized assessments that place learners on continua through qualitative criteria (as opposed to norm-referenced tests that rank learners using percentiles). The KeyMath tests, Peabody Individual Achievement Test, and Woodcock-Johnson Tests of Achievement are examples of criterion-referenced assessment.

Criterion-referenced assessments provide valuable information about your learners' strengths and challenges and can inform, for example, your book recommendations for them in one-on-one reading conferences. However, do not share students' results (e.g., text levels) with learners or their families, because doing so creates an unsustainable pattern. Children will invariably share these levels with each other, comparing themselves with peers, and might even develop a fixed mindset around their ability (e.g., only choosing books at their perceived level). Use information from such assessments to help your students build independence. Guiding and supporting your students' learning will be more sustainable when you empower them to make choices for themselves.

DON'T post classroom assessment data. "Last year, my school was super focused on tracking data and meetings, and we as a staff were quickly burned out by it," shared one 8th grade English teacher from Wisconsin in the #SustainableTeaching survey. "Even when staff voiced their concerns, the workload did not change. I believe there was pressure from the district and state to bring data since we are considered a 'school in improvement.'"

The emphasis on quantitative data in school staff meetings inevitably affects the way that teachers use data with students. Because they have become so accustomed to seeing such data in their meetings, many teachers publicly post assessment data in their classrooms—for example, the percentage of students who have mastered standards based on benchmark assessments. In some cases, schools even post standardized assessment data in the hallways. The intentions behind this practice may be grounded in the pursuit of celebrating collective success, but it is yet another way to marginalize some learners. Consider the effect of posting such data on the handful of learners who have not yet achieved "mastery." How will it affect their motivation? And how does individualism unwittingly reveal itself in this type of purported celebration of the group's success?

DO encourage qualitative self-reflection to highlight progress over achievement. Changing the definition of *success* is critical to building sustainable classroom cultures that are humanizing, inclusive, and empowering. Although it may seem intuitive to use quantitative metrics to foster self-reflection, the reality is that most learners simply look at numbers without reflecting qualitatively on their progress. Learners need to connect their efforts to their progress, and such efforts can only be described qualitatively (Pink, 2009). Further, quantitative metrics reinforce a culture of competition in the classroom: kids can't help but create hierarchies in the face of quantitative rankings or letter-based levels.

Qualitative self-reflection offers a sustainable and humanizing alternative. Instead of labeling themselves and others with levels, grades, or numbers, learners identify qualitative strengths, challenges, and next steps when reflecting on learning artifacts. This practice is more equitable because it removes implicit comparisons and dismantles individualistic hierarchies. All learners can reflect on and reach their own conclusions about their progress, without ranking, ordering, or comparing themselves with each other. (We will unpack more tools to support this shift in Chapter 5.)

DON'T center high-scoring voices. Classrooms that value "correctness" reward learners who have high test scores for taking center stage. These students are more often (and more quickly) "right," and therefore are more incentivized to contribute; as a result, learners with low test scores melt into the background, offering fewer contributions.

The predominance of attention given to learners who have the "right" answer is as much cultural as it is pedagogical. Merely telling learners it's OK to be wrong doesn't solve this problem, and it puts the onus on the individual to brave the task of contributing to the class. Instead, explicitly communicate the value of contributions from all members of the class as part of collective learning, cementing cultural conditions within which all learners feel empowered to contribute. Creating pathways for all voices to be heard is one way to do this.

DO find value in all voices, methods, and answers. *Open-ended tasks* (see Chapter 6) are universally designed so that diverse groups of learners can work toward a common goal, albeit in different ways. When all methods have value, all students can contribute to the learning conversation.

"I don't know how to count by 8s," one of my 3rd graders said to me as she was working on an open-ended task that required multiplying by 8. When I asked her what she *did* know how to do, she said she could count by 2s. So, that's what she did, counting by 2s and circling a group every time she found another group of 8. She ended up sharing her method with the class, and just a week later, I witnessed another student using the same method, no doubt inspired by the first student. This is an example of an inclusive and sustainable pedagogical choice that offers learners another pathway to accessing grade-level content.

Implications for Professional Learning

One of the many recommendations Leah Leonard had for cultivating trust, building rapport, and strengthening relationships within a school was "distributed leadership," acknowledging that it took her years to find comfort in sharing the responsibility of leading a school with her colleagues.

"When I look to my right and I look to my left," she said, "I want to see my colleagues. Not when I turn around. I'm not working ahead of them. They're not following me. It's not a leader–follower kind of relationship. I am a colleague of theirs."

Collegial relationships between administrators and teachers dismantle hierarchies and encourage teachers to play an integral role in upholding the sustainability of teaching and learning.

Other #SustainableTeaching respondents expressed a desire for dismantling hierarchy and distributing leadership as much as possible, too. One 7th grade teacher from Utah described the traditional administration hierarchy as "outdated and unsustainable," stressing that it did not support the student population or their interests. Instead, such a structure leaves students "at the mercy of the district" and does not reflect "their student or teacher needs."

Distributed leadership, on the other hand, *requires* sharing the cognitive, spiritual, emotional, and physical demands of teaching with others. This model leverages partnership and regeneration in the process of interdependently sustaining a school.

"I find that the hierarchical, command-and-control decision making that is the wallpaper in many schools (rarely seen or questioned) is debilitating for teachers, but many endure it as if it is inevitable," shared a high school teacher from Texas. "Many leadership team members (and their bosses) make curricular, pedagogical, and programmatic decisions and mandates that are ill-informed . . . and have significant consequences for teaching and learning." Educators need to make intentional choices to dismantle hierarchy and build collegial relationships among administrators, coaches, and teachers. This can be done through building common visions and making decisions through consensus.

 Distributed leadership encourages teachers to step up and step back at various times, regenerating their energy supply when necessary.

Create a Common Vision for Teaching

"Most mission statements are cliché-filled, adult-focused nonsense," shared Friedrika (Fritzi) Robinson, an elementary school teacher from Rhode Island. "Getting to the school's core by purposefully analyzing and developing a quality mission statement can be a great way to start establishing cultural sustainability."

Empowering individuals to operate with autonomy does not mean allowing teachers to do whatever they please, which would create inconsistent and inequitable learning environments. Within a collectivist approach, teacher autonomy starts with everyone in the school operating with a clear, shared vision for teaching and learning.

Start with guiding questions. A collectivist vision must reflect the voices of all within the collective. This does not mean that every idea makes it into the vision, but rather that the development of the collective vision is an inclusive and transparent process.

Starting with questions is both inclusive and informative. Welcoming ideas from teachers provides coaches and school leaders with insight into their mindsets, philosophies, and background knowledge. Take, for instance, the following questions related to curriculum and pedagogy:

- How do you differentiate or personalize learning?
- What does it mean to be "autonomous" as an educator?
- What is the purpose of assessment in the classroom?
- How do you know when technology is used well?

I used these questions when building a vision with my 3rd grade team (see Figure 2.5). I gave my colleagues time to reflect on the questions, encouraging them to bring their lived experiences and teaching preferences to the conversation. We looked for commonalities among responses and grouped them together on sticky notes. This raised points of both convergence and divergence

FIGURE 2.5

Building a Vision for Teaching

Guiding Question	Vision Statement	Action Steps
How do you differentiate or personalize learning?	Learning is differentiated through a variety of student groupings, activities, lessons, and projects to encompass various learning preferences driven by student choice and interest.	• Plan units using backward design. • Incorporate choice into curriculum to promote agency and autonomy. • Collaborate around student outcomes (e.g., examining work, building rubrics, lesson study, common assessments).
What does it mean to be "autonomous" as an educator?	An autonomous educator has a clear destination, with freedom to use individual teaching style and lesson planning to chart their path. Educators set up classrooms based on their personality and the needs of their students.	• Be transparent and use collaboration structures to our benefit. • Align on clear outcomes (i.e., "destination") and assessments. • Plan units using backward design. • Stick to the plan to maintain consistency. Use the must do/may do in unit plans to identify critical activities, tasks, or lessons that must be covered.
What is the purpose of assessment in the classroom?	At the start, assessment is intended to develop a baseline and a plan. Students use it to learn, grow, and reflect; teachers use it to demonstrate and celebrate growth and to plan for future teaching.	• Conduct benchmark assessments guided by the curriculum map. • Conduct common assessments (e.g., Singapore Math unit assessments, on-demand writing tasks) and reflect on these as a team. • Use common rubrics that are skill-based, not activity-based.
How do you know when technology is used well?	Technology promotes choice, bolstering student autonomy and broadening the audience to which children can make their learning visible.	• Include technological pedagogy in discussions of student outcomes. • Experiment with applications on the iPads. • Allow for educators to exercise autonomy so we can learn through experimentation.

within the team. Addressing divergence does not necessarily mean trying to get everyone on the same page about every minute detail. Instead, it means deciding where divergence and convergence are appropriate and sustainable. Bear in mind that you and your school can choose guiding questions that relate to your school's pedagogical or cultural needs to build a collectivist vision.

Synthesize the results into statements. After grouping sticky notes and finding points of convergence, we created vision statements as a team, using the "headlines" thinking routine from *Project Zero* (Ritchhart et al., 2011). In this routine, participants create a statement of about 15 to 20 words that summarizes an idea. In this case, the "headline" became a vision statement encompassing how we converged around each question.

Ratify the vision. After creating vision statements, all members of the group must ratify them. Note that the vision statements in Figure 2.5 are broad enough that teachers have opportunities for voice and choice in the day-to-day workings of their classrooms, while still establishing some boundaries around what sustainable, humanizing, and high-quality teaching can look like. Part of ratifying the vision is identifying action steps for how the team can collectively realize its vision; like the statements, action steps should allow for divergence in teaching style as appropriate.

Revisit the vision regularly. Your collective vision for teaching and learning should not be fixed but revisited regularly to ensure that the vision is serving sustainable teaching. School visions are more than just words on a page, as Fritzi suggested; they should be your North Star, creating common purpose and engaging all stakeholders in authentic care around the vision. The collective development of a vision ensures this authentic care.

It does not, however, ensure consistency, which is essential to achieving your school vision. The goal of consistency is to ensure that all teachers and classrooms are collectively working toward the school's vision so that all students in the school receive the same quality experience, and students at each grade level learn the same skills. Similarly, communications with families should reflect that consistent experience so that families do not perceive inequity or competition among classes and grade levels. Although teaching styles, experiences, and day-to-day plans differ, learning objectives, formative and summative assessments, rubrics, and key vocabulary should be identical so that teachers can measure learning in a valid and reliable way. Commitment to consistency also ensures that teachers feel heard, supported, and in the loop. Revisiting the vision regularly reinforces the consistency that preserves equity and pluralism, without creating unsustainable uniformity.

Make Decisions Through Consensus

Just as developing a collective vision does not require everyone to agree on every detail, consensus does not require universal agreement. Making decisions based on consensus can be challenging, though, when you know that not everyone will agree on everything.

Fist to Five is a widely known consensus-building tool where participants within a group rank their agreement with a proposal from a fist (zero) to five fingers. For some decisions, any ranking from 1 to 5 communicates an acknowledgement of and consent to the proposal, and rankings signal a level of excitement or willingness to lead: a 1 might convey skepticism of the plan or unwillingness to lead its implementation, while a 4 or 5 signals enthusiasm and a desire to lead.

A fist clearly signals a firm disagreement with the plan. You might ask participants to be prepared to propose alternative solutions or actions if they use a fist to respond to a proposal. This technique has the benefit of leading to a consensus decision if those who are not on board are unable to offer a viable alternative. Their dissent is acknowledged, and all voices are heard.

Allowing any individual to veto a schoolwide policy or decision could be a slippery slope to unsustainability. Your school team will have to decide how to handle a situation when you have participants who stand in firm disagreement. In fact, how to use the Fist to Five tool might be the first item on which you build consensus. Perhaps your team will decide that if you reach a certain threshold of fists, the resolution or proposal will not pass. If, for example, almost half of your community is in firm disagreement with a decision or initiative, it might be wise to make changes to the original proposal before implementing it. Ultimately, the way your school builds consensus will be up to you. The most important thing is to make sure that this decision-making process helps everyone feel invested and heard when making decisions. Consensus decision making can be a vulnerable process, opening up the possibility

> Committing to consensus building means sharing power, which can be scary. To reach sustainability, educators must be willing to let some things go.

for uncertainty, cognitive dissonance, and perhaps even conflict. But it is also the more sustainable choice, slowing down decision making so that all feel empowered to contribute to the collective.

Seeing the Gestalt

Progress toward sustainability in schools is only possible when teachers create the conditions in which collectivism is possible in classrooms. Sustainable teaching leads to sustained learning, which means the collective classroom community plays a role in ensuring learning sticks and persists beyond individual lessons or units. Learning becomes a part of a collective consciousness that compounds with each new learning experience.

In a network of learners, it is not the nodes themselves but the connections between the nodes that make the whole—the collective—so much greater than the sum of its parts. These connections sustain classrooms, allowing all learners—including the teacher—to share in the energy demands of learning in the classroom. A collectivist classroom or school culture creates an environment where learners can witness and harness their own empowerment, which further enhances sustainability.

Chapter Summary

Teachers cannot sustain learning on their own. Educators derive the energy necessary for sustaining learning in classrooms through the relationships they build with students and with each other. An interdependent, authentically caring collectivist classroom is necessary for sustainable teaching; the connections that form between learners and teachers power classrooms. Recognizing this allows educators to redefine classrooms as networks of learners with both gifts and challenges, dismantling cultures of competition and creating a culture within which learners can witness their own power and leverage it to help sustain learning in the classroom.

STOP AND REFLECT

Identify some action steps you can take to shift toward collectivist classroom and professional learning cultures.

- **Amplify:** Which sustainable practices are you already implementing that you want to keep or increase?
- **Alter:** What do you want to change or stop entirely?
- **Activate:** Which new practices would you like to implement to work toward sustainability?

3

Empowerment over Control

ESSENTIAL QUESTION: Where does power originate?

Conventional narratives around teachers and teaching, amplified through the media, often undermine educator humanity, collectivism, and empowerment. Take, for instance, even the most positive portrayals of teachers in *Mr. Holland's Opus* (Herek, 1995) and *Freedom Writers* (LaGravenese, 2007). In both films, the central protagonists all but give up their personal lives for teaching. At one point in *Mr. Holland's Opus*, Glenn Holland's wife suggests that he cares more about his teaching than he does their family. Many teachers have likely experienced this situation with their partners—I know I have. Teachers' work tends to consume them, and many models for "great teachers" put their work as educators above all else.

At one point in *Freedom Writers,* Erin Gruwell, played by Hilary Swank, confronts a student for his lack of attendance and self-assessment, saying, "I am not letting you fail. Even if that means coming to your house every night until you finish the work. I see who you are. Do you understand me? I can see you. And you are not failing."

On one hand, believing in students and ensuring their success can be helpful and humanizing. On the other hand, threatening to show up at a student's house to ensure their success could be construed as a violation of trust, an invasion of privacy, and a breach of teacher–student boundaries. Such stories are rampant in American pop culture, however, contributing to a pervasive narrative of teacher saviorism and martyrdom: teachers must do "whatever it takes" to help students succeed, despite lacking the power to solve systemic problems on their own.

I, too, have felt the pressure of these expectations, especially with the students who have challenged me the most over the years. I am reminded of a student I taught for two years, from 4th to 5th grade, who was witty, energetic, and charismatic. But he struggled with self-regulation, often falling into fits of rage, even throwing objects or destroying parts of my classroom. When he was sent to therapeutic day school for bringing a knife to school, my heart broke. I wept in the nurse's office, in part because of the heaviness of the situation, but also because I felt like I had failed. I had created an individualized curriculum for him, advocated for push-in support, and spent lunches with him to build a relationship. None of it was enough—and that is because I was only one human, imperfect and limited by very real constraints.

It is not a teacher's job to "save" children, despite the conventional narratives. Martyrdom and saviorism exist in relation to each other, differing only in shades of meaning: *martyrdom* requires self-sacrifice, and *saviorism* is the desire to act as a hero. These concepts create an insidious pressure for teachers to give tirelessly of themselves—to bend until they break. Ideas of martyrdom and saviorism are grounded in patriarchal, white supremacy culture (Okun, 2022) and exacerbated by a culture of misogyny that pervades the education system. Teaching is—as it has been historically—a female-dominated profession; approximately 80 percent of public school teachers identify as female (National Center for Education Statistics, 2021).

Women in the United States are commonly expected to give of themselves without the expectation of reciprocity—to act in service of their families, their communities, and their country. It is seen as a woman's duty to be subservient, to not speak up when things are hard. As one 6th grade teacher from rural Minnesota observed, women, in general, are continually tasked to do "more without proper materials or resources." This inequity is exacerbated in an undervalued, female-dominated profession such as teaching. Teachers who attempt to draw boundaries—from asking for more time or declining to be on additional committees—are viewed as "guilty of 'not caring about the kids.'"

Paula Smeltekop, a classroom teacher and media specialist in Illinois, echoed this sentiment, saying that "teachers, librarians, secretaries, nurses—all of these careers in which women were the primary people" were "easy for people to bash. . . . It feels like people are, like, it's just a bunch of women babysitting." The gender pay gap, coupled with teachers' historically low wages, validates this concern.

During the COVID-19 pandemic, many parents identified a need for child-care while children were learning from home; their livelihoods depended on having their kids in school—and, as we know, childcare is not a guaranteed ben-efit in the United States. Although the needs of parents should not supersede teachers' right to safe and healthy working conditions, teachers' self-advocacy for safety was minimized, and children were used to coerce teachers into work-ing in unsafe conditions. Unfortunately, instead of challenging the systems that prevent parents from accessing affordable childcare, critics of the situation made teachers an easy, visible target: they were "lazy" and simply did not want to work. Such narratives are not only unfair but also contribute to the culture of abuse of teachers. In sum, teachers were blamed, abused, and held responsible for societal and systemic faults—all of which were out of their control.

Control Is Unsustainable

Cultures that are subtractive in nature rely on control to maintain assimila-tive practices. Although often effective in maintaining the status quo, this con-trol is ultimately unsustainable. It requires too much energy to micromanage people and assimilate them into a uniform culture. Attempts to micromanage and control teachers and learners also create unproductive conflict. Teachers and learners who feel their agency being taken away will resist, sometimes in subtle ways, but other times in overt ways.

"Teacher autonomy is quickly disappearing," a high school English teacher from Nevada shared with me. "That stems from hard curriculum maps, par-ents who think they know better, admin opinions, and new state [or] local laws. I don't feel I'm always allowed to get to know my students and then plan accordingly."

Notice how shifts toward humanity, collectivism, and empowerment exist in a symbiotic relationship. The desire to industrialize curriculum stems in part from a desire to control standardized test scores. This in turn results in controlling pedagogy, limiting the autonomy of teachers and creat-ing cultures where teachers feel neither supported nor empowered to meet learners where they are.

In the #SustainableTeaching survey, one in five teachers expressed that teacher agency, autonomy, or voice was imperative in creating sustainable schools. Many said this in response to a perceived *lack* of teacher voice and agency within their schools, which has clearly affected teacher morale and retention. Teachers who feel a lack of autonomy will be less engaged in their work and less likely to find the intrinsic motivation to push through challenges (Pink, 2009).

Administrators or school systems that try to systematize and control teaching chip away at teacher agency. Harmful narratives around teacher saviorism and martyrdom make it even easier to control teachers by leveraging both compliance and guilt. As a result, teachers feel disempowered to be innovative, solve problems, and otherwise share in the demands of sustaining learning within their schools and districts.

The dissolution of teacher agency in turn creates classrooms that diminish learner agency. Because teachers constantly feel threatened with losing their jobs—and by proxy their salary and health insurance—they are left with no choice but to conform and submit to attempts to control pedagogy. Because they feel pressure to industrialize learning, they inadvertently pressure students to produce predetermined products of learning, which not only counteracts efforts to create validating and pluralistic school cultures but also limits learner agency. Instead of enabling sustained, meaningful, and relevant learning that transfers into students' lives, such compliance practices are likely to make learning unsustainable.

The alternative to controlling teachers, learners, and learning is not for administrators and coaches to "empower" teachers and for teachers to "empower" learners. This interpretation of empowerment is paternalistic, implying that teachers and learners need someone else to bestow power upon them for them to access it. Instead, the alternative is to create supportive conditions within which teachers and learners alike can manifest their agency, sharing in the demands of sustaining learning in schools.

Creating Supportive Conditions for Agency

Classrooms that create supportive conditions for empowerment are agentive and innovative, so that learners can share the energy demands of learning. This shared responsibility for learning offers a path to sustainability; it does not require one individual or a small group of individuals to deplete their energy reserves for learning to happen in the classroom.

Instead, through the partnerships that exist within a collectivist classroom, all contribute to learning through their agency. Everyone's energy expenditure is more efficient: when some learners need to regenerate and replenish their energy reserves, others can step forward and expend more. Empowering learners to make decisions also simplifies teachers' workloads, allowing them to do more in partnership with learners than they could by themselves. Empowering learners and teachers does not mean granting them unbridled independence; it simply means creating the conditions in which students learn to make choices within agreed-upon boundaries. This reiterates the importance of creating these expectations through a strong vision, as discussed in Chapter 2.

Agency

Centering teachers as saviors or martyrs in schools reflects deficit-based thinking—assuming that there is something inherently wrong with students and that they must be "saved" by teachers. It is also paternalistic in nature. Teachers cannot *give* learners power; instead, they can create conditions within which learners can witness their own power and exercise it. "The idea that one individual or school can give students 'a life' emanates from a problematic savior complex that results in making students, their varied experiences, their emotions, and the good in their communities invisible" (Emdin, 2016, p. 20).

> Creating the conditions for learner empowerment leverages partnerships with learners and enables them to regenerate their energy reserves, while also simplifying teachers' workloads.

Shifting toward agency means considering the learning environment and determining which tools, structures, and systems incentivize learners to make choices and witness a power that already exists within them. This shift requires reframing teachers' roles: their purpose is not to fix learners or dictate their choices but to help students learn how to exercise their agency—a transferable skill that will serve them outside of the walls of the classroom.

Innovation

Agentive school cultures are primed for innovation. Respondents to the #SustainableTeaching survey described innovation as both sustainable and unsustainable—the difference seeming to hinge on *how* innovation is encouraged in schools.

The unwillingness of some teachers to innovate is an unsustainable practice; for teaching to be sustainable, educators must be willing to engage with sustainability as a process. Teachers must be prepared to evaluate current needs and change their practices in response. But it is worth exploring and acknowledging the existence of conditions that contextualize teachers' hesitance to innovate.

One high school teacher from Oklahoma suggested that the education system itself "is not meant to handle true innovation . . . due to the overemphasis on testing and 'sameness' of curriculum." A middle school personalized learning coach from Texas described an expectation of innovating for innovation's sake, which is "difficult to maintain."

Just as schools need to create genuine cultures of caring (Valenzuela, 1999), they must implement genuine cultures of innovation. School cultures that are innovating aesthetically might have shiny new textbooks or fancy new gadgets, creating a façade of innovation—a façade that is ultimately unsustainable when it runs out of energy. Either the new textbooks sit on the shelf untouched or teachers experience *initiative burnout,* in which their hearts, minds, and bodies can no longer tolerate anything new.

Teachers *want* to innovate; that much is clear from responses to the #SustainableTeaching survey. One STEM teacher from California noted:

> Innovative teachers want avenues to share with others. It's what keeps the creative juices flowing. A school district should develop means for staff members to share innovative tools and technologies across schools. Innovative teachers shouldn't be contained within the four walls of their classroom. It's stifling.

I have visceral memories of collaborating with my first teaching team in the suburbs of Chicago. We were more than colleagues: we were lab partners, critical friends, and comrades. We held weekly meetings to reflect on our implementation of one-to-one devices, sharing not only our successes but also our failures so that we could benefit from the collective wisdom that results from being vulnerable with our practice. The result was a sustainable culture of

 Sustainability results from teachers feeling safe to take risks and make mistakes, energizing them to continue to be curious about new ways to approach learning.

collaboration and innovation that kept me curious about how I could best meet the evolving needs of my learners.

The barrier to innovation most cited by survey respondents, however, wasn't necessarily access to pathways for sharing; it was the time required to do so. One high school teacher reflected:

> They believe me to be a highly qualified and effective teacher who innovates in the classroom and holds progressive views of education, which they aspire to, but do not understand how I can accomplish all this during my contract day.

Time—or the lack of it—was a common theme, with respondents offering a handful of ideas for tangible reforms that would allow teachers to innovate within the confines of the school day. For example, protecting teachers' planning and professional learning time "must be maintained in order to promote quality planning, collaborative grading, innovative idea sharing, and even work/life balance," said a high school teacher from Iowa. "Humans are wired to connect with other humans, and without time dedicated to connecting with one another to find common ground around our daily tasks, we become less effective."

Further, the approach to innovation must be intentional and measured. Innovations should be grounded in authentic purpose, building on the assets of students and solving problems related to equity, access, and opportunity gaps. As one high school teacher in Illinois noted, "We cannot be innovative all the time"; bear in mind that it is OK to take breaks from innovation. It's OK to stop, reflect, and celebrate everything that *is* working in classrooms. Celebrating successes is both energizing and sustainable.

STOP AND REFLECT

- How effectively are your classroom and school creating the conditions in which learners can feel empowered?
- In what ways is your classroom *agentive,* creating the conditions within which learners can learn to make choices?
- What steps have you taken to be *purposefully innovative* in your teaching?

Pedagogies for Learner Empowerment

Creating conditions for learners to exercise their agency does not necessitate an overhaul of your curriculum and teaching. It's nearly impossible to make such significant shifts overnight. Not only is it too much work, but most teachers do not possess the power to move the needle as far as they might want to. For better or worse, teachers need to work within the boundaries set by their administrators and schools.

Consider building learner agency as a mindful journey, with each step manifesting as incremental shifts in pedagogy. Over time, these efforts compound, creating agentive and innovative classroom cultures. Think of the inputs to learner agency in terms of three categories: building on learners' gifts, explicitly teaching executive function skills, and embedding social-emotional learning (SEL).

Building on Learners' Gifts

Creating conditions for learner agency includes ensuring that learners can take risks, make mistakes, and find their footing when they fall. This process begins with holding learners' humanity sacred through culturally sustaining pedagogy and preserving their identities while helping them access new skills that will deepen their understanding of themselves, others, and the world around them. Sustaining student identities requires amplifying and building on the gifts they bring to the classroom. One 3rd grade teacher from Illinois described "finding a curriculum or activities that match the needs and funds of knowledge of students" as essential to creating "success in our students."

The term *funds of knowledge* (Moll et al., 1992) refers to the strengths that lie within the lived experiences of all students. Too many classrooms are places that fail to appreciate all student gifts equally. American schooling disproportionately values reading, writing, mathematics, and science above other content and skill areas; mathematics and science no doubt make the cut due to economic demand in STEM fields. These four academic areas are also disproportionately valued because they are tested subjects—once again feeding the testing-industrial complex.

You might not be able to change what is tested in your school or state, but you can find ways to amplify learner gifts in historically tested subjects, creating the conditions for learner empowerment. You can do this by varying the modalities for demonstrating understanding, helping learners personalize their process, and making progress visible with qualitative assessment.

Vary modalities for demonstrating understanding. Differentiated Instruction, a framework for teaching championed by education leader Carol Ann Tomlinson (1999), allows for modification of content, process, product, or learning environment to connect with students in equitable and accessible ways. Setting up different modalities for learners to demonstrate their understanding falls under differentiating process or product.

Some teachers vary requirements for learning products by incorporating students' interests or providing different ways to communicate understanding—drawing pictures, writing songs or raps, making videos. This type of flexibility allows learners to communicate in a manner that empowers them and makes them feel successful, especially students who experience barriers when writing. Varying modalities, however, should not create ways for students to avoid reading and writing altogether, and every option must truly allow students to demonstrate understanding of the learning objective.

For instance, writing a song collaboratively about how to multiply and divide fractions using the standard algorithm may help students recall the procedure, but the product does not ensure students have a conceptual understanding of this skill or that they are able to do it consistently with accuracy. When the means for demonstrating understanding does not align with the demands of the actual skill, it may create an unintended barrier for students in the long run. Providing varied modalities for demonstrating understanding is only sustainable if it results in clear evidence of deep, meaningful, transferable student learning.

Some teachers modify instructional processes to center their students' gifts. For example, some students may need concrete manipulatives like base-10 blocks or number discs to calculate; others might draw pictures or use algorithms. Regardless of the process used, allowing learners to choose is empowering because they can experience competence using a tool that works for them.

Help students personalize their process through goal setting. Teaching learners to set their own goals allows them to personalize their process, leading to learner empowerment and sustainability. When teachers set goals on behalf of learners, it creates dependence, sending the implicit message that students cannot do this on their own. (It's also a lot of work that is difficult for one person to keep up.) For post-assessment self-reflection and goal setting, I use a very simple framework. Students identify **strengths** ("I succeeded by . . ."), **challenges** ("I am still working on . . ."), and **next steps** ("Next time, I will . . ."). This simple framework can be applied to different contexts or subjects.

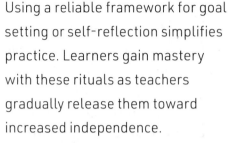

Using a reliable framework for goal setting or self-reflection simplifies practice. Learners gain mastery with these rituals as teachers gradually release them toward increased independence.

You can also use self-reflection questions at the end of a lesson, either as a general class discussion or for individual reflection. Doing this regularly creates a ritual around self-reflection that in turn becomes self-sustaining as a regenerative tool for enhancing learner self-awareness and continuous goal setting.

For long-term projects, I recommend providing students with blank calendars. Project-based learning can often feel unsustainable and overly complex at the outset. Goal-setting calendars help learners break down projects into bite-sized pieces and make project-based learning more sustainable. Using a tool like this also builds executive function skills in learners, teaching a transferable skill that will sustain learning beyond the classroom.

Make progress visible with qualitative assessment. At the end of one school year, my students were looking through their portfolios and journals and reflecting. It was humbling to look around the room, listening to the awe and wonder in their voices as they saw how much they had learned that year. Students had as many as six math journals—formerly blank pages—filled with their thinking. Some had three or four "thinking journals," likewise blank when the year started but now filled with their responses to primary sources, stories they had read, and (for some) big feelings they had had on tough days.

One of my students commented, "I used to only see the bad things in my work," but they could now "see the good things, too." This student's journey in my 3rd grade classroom was long and sometimes arduous, going from crawling under their desk in the first months of school to avoid challenging tasks to being a consistently active member of our learning community, sharing methods for open-ended math tasks and excerpts of their stories in whole-group reflections.

Centering quantitative data or letter grades takes away from student empowerment, especially for the most vulnerable learners. Putting letter grades or point totals, which are often deficit-framing, on this student's work would have been disempowering. Assessment should entail telling the story of students' learning journey, centering their gifts and using those gifts as tools for taking on new challenges. Assessment should not further subtract from students' self-concept for the purpose of compliance or control. (See Chapter 5 for more exploration of sustainable assessment practices.)

I have yet to find a more effective means of qualitative assessment of educational progress than portfolios and journals. They are simple, they are dynamic, and they allow learners to easily go back in time—to compare what they used to do and think with what is happening in the present. Seeing growth in this way is inherently personalized, humanizing, and empowering—and it's good for *all* learners.

Portfolios and journals act as containers for evidence of student learning that learners can maintain with little support, simplifying teachers' jobs.

Teaching Executive Function

Empowering students requires more than encouragement, validation, and freedom to make choices. Students need to learn *how* to make choices.

"Do you know what an executive does?" I ask my students. They've often heard the term before, and we'll discuss how the president is part of the executive branch of government, or how an executive at a company is usually in charge of making important decisions.

"Well," I continue, "you have an executive in your body, too. It makes lots of decisions for your body. Do you know where it is?"

They eventually realize I am talking about the brain, and I use this as an entry point for teaching about executive function. Using technical terms is both empowering and educative for even the youngest learners. Ellin Keene and Susan Zimmermann (1997) encourage teachers to use the term *metacognition* to teach kids how to think about their thinking.

I have taught students that there are three basic components of executive function: cognitive flexibility, inhibitory control, and working memory (Belsky, n.d.). *Cognitive flexibility* is the ability to think flexibly, *inhibitory control* is the ability to manage temptations, and *working memory* enables holding multiple things in one's mind at once. However, you need to do more than teach students definitions of these terms. You must contextualize the concepts by identifying authentic situations where students need to use executive function skills and tools. These situations can be fictional or real, based on students' lives or your classroom.

Cognitive flexibility. Learners struggle with flexible thinking in all sorts of situations, like when something does not turn out the way they had hoped or when a friend acts in a manner they did not expect. Cognitive *inflexibility* might surface when students come to an obstacle while reading, writing, or problem solving. Not only do they need to be able to notice these roadblocks, they also need to have tools to respond.

Stephanie Madrigal and Michelle Garcia Winner (2009) authored a series of books featuring Superflex, a protagonist who takes on Unthinkables—villains like Rock Brain, Glassman, and Worry Wall—who coax people to fall into rigid thinking. Learners can relate to these characters when working through inflexible thinking.

The Unthinkables characters serve multiple purposes. First, they depersonalize the experiences connected with inflexible thinking. Instead of a fixed trait (i.e., "I am an inflexible person"), the trait is viewed as a state of being (i.e., "Sometimes Rock Brain gets into my mind and tells me to be inflexible") or something that is happening to them as opposed to a part of who they are. This understanding engenders a growth mindset (Dweck, 2008) in learners, helping them see that they do, in fact, have some control over their own flexibility. It also allows them to *name* what is happening to them. Often, learners lack the vocabulary to name how they are feeling or what they are experiencing. Once learners can name the source of their inflexibility, they can tame it; providing them with examples helps with this process.

Examples like the Unthinkables stories also help students build a strategy toolbox. Garcia Winner has also published a social-thinking curriculum (2002, 2008) that offers a diverse array of tools and strategies for building cognitive flexibility. As learners begin to know themselves better, they will identify the strategies that work best for them. You might start by presenting your class with a scenario like the following:

> Emily got to her lunch table and realized that both seats next to her best friend were taken. She had checked in with her friend earlier, and they said they'd sit together. What should Emily do?

Students might offer a variety of strategies to respond to this situation, from taking deep breaths to sharing her feelings with her friends. Discussing the scenario with students allows you to introduce the concept of *self-talk*, a productive strategy for helping learners build language around self-regulation (Fahy, 2014). You can ask students, "What might Emily say to herself in her mind?" and have pairs of students discuss their ideas and write them on a sticky note.

These notes can be combined on a board or anchor chart and reviewed with the whole class. Your students might have suggestions like these:

- This didn't turn out the way I expected, but this is a small problem. I don't need to have a big reaction to this.
- Maybe if I ask to sit next to my friend, they will let me.
- I didn't get to sit by my friend today, but maybe I can sit near her tomorrow.

This activity provides an opportunity for students to practice pausing, reflecting, and finding language on their own so that they are ready to practice self-talk in other situations. This practice ultimately supports sustainability in the classroom because it empowers learners to solve problems themselves, only calling upon teachers for support and advice when necessary.

Inhibitory control. Although inhibitory control might be described as the ability to resist temptations, it also incorporates the ability to regulate emotions and manage reactions to emotions, or *managing impulsivity*. It is empowering and validating to know that everyone in the classroom is allowed to experience a full range of emotions, pleasant and unpleasant. In Emily's scenario, inhibitory control and cognitive flexibility work hand in hand to help Emily handle the situation productively.

Learners experience temptations all the time in the classroom, such as the temptation to run across the classroom and grab materials first (even though there are more than enough materials for everyone) or to rush through less-preferred activities. Learners need to *see* that inhibitory control might be a challenge; the challenge must be made visible to them.

Teachers often address challenges with inhibitory control that arise in the classroom in an unsustainable manner: they are putting out fires (for lack of a better term) and responding to unexpected behaviors in a reactive way (Garcia Winner, 2002, 2008). However, taking a more proactive and sustainable approach to building stamina for inhibitory control makes kids partners in the process of managing themselves within the classroom.

One way to address unexpected behavior proactively is to engage learners in practicing *mindfulness*—the art of noticing. Mindfulness is more than basic meditation, although it could entail students closing their eyes and doing a "body scan," directing their attention to different parts of their bodies and noticing sensations in their legs, bellies, hearts, necks, and arms. Mindfulness also includes noticing what your body does with various emotional responses. RULER's Mood Meter (Brackett, 2019) and Zones of Regulation (Kuypers, 2011) are two frameworks for identifying emotions with mindfulness work.

Learners need access to tools that aid them in self-regulation and practicing inhibitory control. Consider incorporating a sensory or physical regulation area in your classroom, where learners have access to fidgets or other gross-motor tools (e.g., foam rollers, exercise balls, stretchy bands). Perhaps your flexible seating options could include wobble stools or wiggly chairs. Note that these tools can quickly become unsustainable and unwieldy if used poorly. Learners must be taught how to employ them appropriately; as you introduce them, set classroom agreements as a class around their use. These conversations, paired with explicit modeling, will support sustainability in the long run by empowering learners to give their bodies and hearts what they need to feel successful and regulated in the classroom.

Teaching executive function skills and noticing proactively frames this learning in a positive way, making learners partners in the process of managing behavior.

Working memory. Working memory is just one component of executive function, though it is the one that comes to mind most often. When I talk with kids about working memory, I describe it to them as the ability to hold multiple things in your mind at once. To build your students' working memory, you must explicitly teach them routines that support the skill.

Rehearsal can support working memory growth. I begin teaching rehearsal when building routines with learners. Although I use visual checklists to support building routines, I also have students practice recalling multistep directions—after all, visual checklists are supposed to be a scaffold, not a permanent tool. I cue them by asking them to count the steps on their fingers while I say them aloud. I also ask them to "rehearse" the steps in their minds while I'm saying them. I make sure to speak slowly, leaving space in between each direction, to give students a moment to repeat it in their minds. When I finish sharing the steps, students turn and talk with a neighbor.

There are also project-management tools that can help build students' working memory. A simple calendar might help learners chunk long-term projects or set daily goals for projects. Students might use a Get Ready–Doing–Done template (Jacobsen & Ward, 2016; see Figure 3.1), working with either a virtual board or a trifold with sticky notes, to organize their work and follow their progress.

More involved scaffolds for working memory—checklists, colored clocks, personal timers—help students cultivate an awareness of time. The implicit

FIGURE 3.1

Get Ready–Doing–Done Chart

This chart shows a student's progress on a tiny home project.

Get Ready	Doing	Done
What are your steps? What will you need to do to complete your passion project?	*Move steps here as you're working on them.*	*Move steps here when you're done with them.*

Get Ready
- Write paragraph about how tiny homes help the environment
- Make the showcase for my tiny home model and for the printed-out paragraph
- Make tiny home model
- Make little number pieces to put by each system in my tiny home and make sure to number the paragraph where I talk about that system and how it has changed between the tiny home and the normal-sized home
- Make paragraphs separate from the other paragraph about each system in the tiny home model
- Make structure for the info piece

Doing
- Make presentation
- Make tiny home design

Done
- Purpose
- How do systems evolve, change, and grow?
- Research the history of housing
- Identify the major systems in homes
- Read "Tiny House Villages in Seattle— An Efficient Response to Our Homelessness Crisis"
- Read "Tiny Houses—Not a Big Enough Solution"
- List materials for tiny home model

goal for all these tools is for learners to use them independently. Doing so builds executive function skills and teaches students to be accountable to themselves—yet another transferable skill that will serve them outside the classroom. This also benefits you, the teacher: the less time you devote to tasks that create learned helplessness or dependence in learners, the more time you have for tasks that are truly worth your time.

Embedding SEL and Executive Function

"The way an individual knows themself and organizes themself is way more important than any content," a middle school English teacher from Singapore shared. "By prioritizing SEL, learners can learn anything! They look after [themselves] first. This then makes any learning thereafter sustainable."

This teacher not only makes the case for centering executive function skills in classrooms but also emphasizes that *every* teacher should be teaching executive function. A commonly unsustainable mindset—especially in middle and high school—is that teachers are experts in disseminating content. The reality is, however, that educators at all levels need to teach *children,* not content.

The emphasis on content harkens back to the industrialization of teaching and explains one reason current approaches to teaching are largely unsustainable. Neglecting SEL effaces learners' humanity—and results in lost opportunities for building learners' and teachers' energy reserves for learning. Creating conditions for learner agency requires teachers to prioritize learners' humanity and in turn optimizes classrooms for sustainable agency.

Providing students with an understanding of executive function and tools to build them can take the form of minilessons embedded within core teaching (see Figure 3.2 for examples). While teaching students about a specific writing strategy, show them how to use a timer to set goals related to writing stamina. Students can learn about making choices by using erasable checklists that help them manage their workload. Perhaps they have several outstanding tasks, such as completing workbook pages, correcting quiz answers, and playing a math game. Teaching them how to make a checklist takes some of the

Partnering with learners to develop scenarios that build executive function skills makes less work for the teacher while giving students opportunities to identify specific situations where they could use these skills.

FIGURE 3.2

Tools to Develop Executive Function Skills

Tool	Description
Must do/ may do	Create a two-column chart that summarizes universal tasks all learners must complete. In one column, make a checklist of "must do" tasks learners can use to monitor their progress. In the other column, list "may do" choices related to academic content. Consider incorporating options that align with students' various academic needs. Include a review or remediation activity, an activity that provides more practice on currently taught skills, and an enrichment activity. Coach learners on how to make choices that fit their readiness level.
Choice boards	Choice boards are a scaffold to help students learn how to make choices on their own. Start with a limited number (one to three) of choices, and slowly add more as the year progresses. Accounting for various readiness levels is imperative; coaching learners to make choices that align with their readiness levels will lead to even more empowerment.
Erasable checklists	Use erasable checklists to track progress toward a long-term project or to keep track of work completion during a single class period. Erasable checklists are suitable for a range of content areas, such as editing in writing or completing multistep problems in math or science.
Goal setting	Break work assignments down into short-, medium-, and long-term goals, monitored using erasable checklists or calendars. Teach students to break down tasks and manage their time. Help students set formal and informal goals. Formal goals might use the SMART framework (i.e., goals that are Specific, Measurable, Actionable, Realistic, and Time-bound). Informal goals might be developed through conversations about goals during morning meeting, as an assignment is being described, or in 5- to 10-minute reflections at the end of every learning block.
Self-reflection	Self-reflection allows learners to identify strengths, challenges, and next steps. Structure time for self-reflection into a variety of situations, such as in response to a single class period, a formative assessment encompassing a period of instructional time, or a summative assessment.

responsibility off you in terms of monitoring their progress while building a transferable skill.

You can also introduce learners to executive function tools during morning meeting if you are an elementary school teacher, or in homeroom if you teach middle or high school. After introducing students to the concepts and presenting them with scenarios to consider, have them create their own scenarios for practicing executive function skills.

Implications for Professional Learning

"When educators don't feel like they belong, there is no way students can feel like they belong," a high school social studies teacher from Oregon shared in the #SustainableTeaching survey. This statement reflects the importance of both identity work and conditions in which teachers feel supported and empowered. Cultures of belonging center teachers' gifts and use protocols for equity of voice, helping them feel seen, heard, and valued. This acknowledgment contributes to a validating and pluralistic culture around professional learning, sustaining inquiry and serving the collective purpose of helping all learners feel seen, heard, and valued in the classroom.

Centering Teacher Gifts

All teachers have gifts to offer. If we are building upon the funds of knowledge students bring to increase their agency, we must offer teachers this same courtesy. How might professional learning change if educators embrace the idea that even teachers who seem the most disgruntled, disengaged, or ineffective have gifts to offer? This does not mean praising mediocre teaching or allowing teachers to sit in complacent discomfort, but rather requires coaches and administrators to identify teachers' strengths so they can use them as tools for growing practice.

It also requires reframing dissenting viewpoints or seemingly "negative" teachers as offering something to the education environment. Teachers don't disengage from teaching just to be difficult. They disengage because despite their efforts—and despite voicing their concerns—nothing seems to change. No one listens, and no one believes them. There is nothing less empowering than feeling invisible and silenced.

When I meet teachers who are resistant to my way of thinking about teaching and learning, or teachers who try to disrupt professional learning, I find that asking them questions can be disarming and even empowering. But the questions must come from a genuine place of wonder, understanding, and belief.

Several coaching models incorporate centering teachers' gifts in the classroom. Charlotte Danielson's Framework for Teaching (2009) has been used throughout the United States to support teacher reflection, collaboration, inquiry, and innovation. Jim Knight, author of *The Impact Cycle* (2018), invites coaches and coachees to first garner a "clear picture of current reality" in the classroom (p. 27), then has teachers set clear goals and gather data to gauge their effectiveness. Coaches can begin the initial conversation on the "current reality" of their classroom by helping teachers identify their gifts.

Protocols for Equity of Voice

Feeling voiceless is ultimately disempowering for teachers. Some are quiet not because they feel they have nothing to offer, but because they feel as though they cannot get a word in. As someone who is learning to take up less space in conversations, I can say with certainty that equity of voice protocols help me, too, be more prudent with what I say and how much airtime I give myself.

Equity of voice protocols can be very simple. Divide the time you have for dialogue by the number of people in the room. Offer each person their allotted amount of time, using a timer to signal when their time is up. If participants do not use all their allotted time, it is reasonable for them to forfeit the remainder or pass on the opportunity to speak entirely. Some groups prefer a discussion norm around stepping up and stepping back, which can be effective—as long as all participants in the group feel comfortable giving and receiving feedback on when individuals are taking up too much space.

Written reflections also provide an avenue for equity of voice. At the end of a meeting or learning lab, I sometimes ask participants to write down a reflection to share with me. This practice allows me to take in feedback that may have gone unsaid due to shyness or a missed opportunity.

Simple equity of voice protocols are more sustainable because they are easy to enact.

Letting Go Allows for Minimalism

In the preceding chapters, we explored how identity work contributes to sustainable teaching, creating a validating and pluralistic classroom, and the value of interdependence and cultures of authentic care for learning in collectivist classrooms. These concepts lay the foundation for examining conditions in which learners feel supported and empowered to make decisions. The mindset shifts I've discussed so far humanize learning, creating space for partnership, healing, and vulnerability in the classroom.

In the absence of humanizing, collectivist, empowering classroom cultures, teachers tend to fill time with activities that neither enrich learning nor help them find sustainability. Do you ever find yourself copying worksheets you will never look at or creating activities to keep kids busy? Shifting toward sustainability and creating the conditions within which learners are empowered to make choices independently enables a minimalist approach to designing learning experiences, eliminating busywork and immersing learners in rich, self-sustaining activities that are worth their time. We'll explore this notion in the context of minimalist curriculum design in the next chapter.

Chapter Summary

Power comes from within. Educators must create the conditions within which learners and teachers alike can connect with their own power, using it to sustain learning in the classroom. Interdependent and authentically caring cultures of learning create the conditions to empower learners and teachers, granting them both opportunities to be agentive and innovative and to leverage their partnership to share in the demands of learning. These conditions also simplify teachers' jobs while enhancing learners' school experiences. Teachers' jobs must be simpler to achieve sustainability. Simplicity allows for a minimalist approach to curriculum design, but this approach will only be successful if learners feel empowered to make choices within a minimalist curriculum.

STOP AND REFLECT

Identify some action steps you can take to create the conditions for learner empowerment.

- **Amplify:** Which sustainable practices are you already implementing that you want to keep or increase?
- **Alter:** What do you want to change or stop entirely?
- **Activate:** Which new practices would you like to implement to work toward sustainability?

4

Minimalism over Maximalism

ESSENTIAL QUESTION: When does doing less provide more?

In Summer 2014, I set my sights on San Francisco, looking for acceptance as an openly queer educator in the wake of the fallout from the marriage equality lesson I mentioned in Chapter 1. I found it as an elementary school teacher in Silicon Valley, working for an emerging educational technology company and network of microschools dedicated to personalized learning.

Our theory for personalization was simple: if every child had an individualized "playlist" of activities, then we could personalize learning at scale and close gaps in achievement. At the outset, it seemed intuitive: the more individualized the curriculum was, the more personalized it would be. Implementation, however, was not quite as simple, and I learned that overindividualizing curriculum has unsustainable consequences (France, 2022).

This approach to personalization fails to create conditions for empowerment. Focusing on fruitful learning, not completing playlist activities, is what builds transferable skills and learner agency. The approach was also overly individualistic. Giving every child their own playlist—so that all students are working on different activities—takes away opportunities for learners to connect with each other. And overindividualizing learning is inequitable, creating access and opportunity gaps and providing some learners content at higher levels than others. Ultimately our efforts produced an industrialized, disempowering, individualistic paradigm, with students on the receiving end of granulated instructional materials, ground into bits and pieces in the form of playlist cards—a bit too much like Côte's futuristic drawing in Figure 1.1.

Creating, monitoring, and assessing individualized learning plans—even in a class of fewer than 20 students—creates an excess of data and a great deal of work, without proportional return on the teacher's time investment. To be constantly running around a classroom putting out fires, clarifying misconceptions, and helping learners is physically, emotionally, and cognitively draining.

Maximalism Is Unsustainable

Overpersonalizing learning is maximalist in nature—too much individualization requires an excess of planning from teachers and produces an excess of data to analyze and act on, both of which lead to burnout. Why is it that educators often believe more is more? Could doing less, perhaps, actually achieve more?

American culture is often defined by excess, and this way of thinking has infiltrated our classrooms. This broader desire for "more" has played an instrumental role in the world's climate crisis, accelerating the extraction and exploitation of natural resources. It is also a culprit in education's climate crisis, unsustainably extracting and exploiting teachers' energy reserves. Maximalism has conditioned educators to believe that the more activities, choices, and data they have—and the faster they accelerate both the consumption of these materials and learning itself—the richer learning will be. But this cannot be true if the methodologies for designing learning experiences burn teachers out and saturate learners.

Maximalism manifests in classrooms in other ways, too, for instance, when we leverage worksheet- and workbook-based pedagogies. After all, the more work students complete, the more learning is happening, right? And the more technology teachers use, the more progressive and cutting-edge they are, right? We should know better, but it's tempting to fall into these traps. In addition, some teachers tend to believe that there is a direct correlation between the amount of time they spend on their jobs and the quality of their teaching, when the reality is quite the contrary.

One in three respondents in the #SustainableTeaching survey identified time as a factor influencing the unsustainability of teaching. Most commonly, respondents described a lack of planning time; others stressed that the sheer number of responsibilities teachers have cannot be accomplished within the confines of an eight-hour workday. A middle school English language arts teacher from Iowa recounted:

> I can't recall a year in which something new wasn't added to my plate. Nothing is taken off. We constantly have to balance what gets priority at any given moment of our day. I typically work until 5:00 p.m.—two and a half hours after contract—to grade papers, input grades, plan, and make parent contacts, and usually have an additional one to two hours of work to do after my children are in bed. This is unsustainable.

It is tempting to succumb to the idea that there will never be enough time in the day. "Teaching is just hard," some will say. "This is what you signed up for." But when will we draw the line? When will we decide that enough is enough and become advocates for teachers to have more sustainable workloads? Until we make the courageous choice that it is, in fact, possible for teachers' workloads to be reduced without negatively affecting student learning, we are resigning ourselves to an unproductive and maximalist mindset that will continue to burn teachers out.

Enacting Minimalism for Simpler Instructional Design

To embrace minimalism in teaching, begin by reiterating this idea: *It's not best practice if it's not sustainable.* This means finding practices that lead to rich learning experiences while keeping curriculum design manageable within a reasonable workweek. Planning as many activities as there are learners in the classroom simply is not sustainable: it cannot be kept up over the course of an entire school year, even if it will theoretically meet all learners where they are. Even planning multiple activities for leveled groups poses challenges for teachers in terms of sustainability. Although classrooms should be engineered with options, this does not necessarily entail planning two to three different lessons for different groups of students over the course of a single learning block.

Taking an intentional and embodied approach to curriculum design makes teachers' jobs simpler without reducing the quality of learning experiences.

A minimalist mindset toward designing learning experiences encourages efficiency by cutting out practices that benefit neither teachers nor students and amplifying practices that are mutually beneficial. Educators can simplify instructional design by being intentional with learning design and taking an embodied approach, as opposed to the disembodied approach that breaks the curriculum down into pieces and industrializes it.

Intentional

In my first years of teaching, I operated without intent, caught in the cycle of assigning, completing, collecting, grading, and returning an excess of meaningless work to students. In addition to this routine reflecting a product-focused mindset toward assessment—which we will explore in the next chapter—it was also maximalist. I had been conditioned to believe that the more activities I had to assess, the more data I would have, and the more feedback kids would get. But the reality is that this excess of activities did not make the learning richer or me a better teacher—it just meant I was working more.

Allysun Sokolowski is an elementary and middle school teacher in Bethesda, Maryland. In our interview for the #SustainableTeaching project, she shared the importance of setting boundaries around workload, describing how she tracks her time:

> I know that if I hit 55 hours a week, I have to stop. I have learned that 55 hours a week is my breaking point. And I can do it once or twice. But after that I get angry and resentful, and I hate what I'm doing.

Allysun stressed that 55 hours might not be a universal number. For another teacher, "it might be 45—or . . . 65 or whatever. You know, it's just a part of . . . that kind of self-feedback."

Setting personal boundaries is essential to finding sustainability—and it is one of the things teachers *can* control in their classrooms. Setting boundaries around time and tasks helps teachers identify and reflect on which responsibilities are essential and which activities or processes create more work without a proportional return on investment. This in turn enables them to be more intentional about planning and preparing to teach.

Being intentional benefits both learners and teachers. When teachers are intentional, they provide activities that promote inquiry, deepen learning, and engage students in rigorous, independent thinking. These same activities are *worth* reviewing and assessing, and they provide relevant data to inform instruction.

Embodied

Approximately 10 percent of teachers in the #SustainableTeaching survey referred to "initiative fatigue." Not only were there too many initiatives in any given year, but the drive behind the initiatives seemed quick to burn out. Then in succeeding years there would be new sets of initiatives, compounding the unsustainability of previous years' initiatives.

"You never really get time to hone your craft," a preschool teacher from New York shared, "because by the time you do, it's over." A kindergarten teacher from Seattle echoed this sentiment:

> None of the curriculum adoptions last for more than a few years, making it impossible to build a craft.... Also, none of the curricula across subjects speak together or enhance each other, which is such a waste of energy and time.

When approaches to curriculum, assessment, instruction, and professional learning are maximalist, there are too many initiatives (often independent of one another) circulating. These circumstances make it difficult for teachers to have time to develop a sense of competence or mastery in any of them, all the while aware that the initiatives they are to follow could change at the drop of a hat.

The maximalist approach affects students, too. When there are too many skills to master, kids become overwhelmed. They cannot keep track of that many skills, and the feeling of being swamped can cause them to disengage and misunderstand the inherent value of what they are learning.

An intentional and embodied approach to district- or schoolwide initiatives means *streamlining* initiatives, creating connections between some and getting rid of nonessential ones. Instructional design benefits from an embodied approach, too, streamlining teachers' work and reducing the amount of time spent planning. This in turn creates space and time for teachers to distribute and use their energy reserves for essential parts of their jobs. It also creates space for learners to make transferable and sustainable connections between new skills, lessons, and academic subjects—lessening the need for teachers to review and reteach already explored concepts. An embodied approach to curriculum allows various programs to "speak together," as the teacher from Seattle characterized it, adding to sustainability efforts.

STOP AND REFLECT

- Are you, in your classroom or school, already embracing minimalist approaches?
- In what ways is your approach to curriculum aligned to learning outcomes and intentionally designed with sustainability in mind?
- What steps have you taken to make instructional design more embodied, drawing connections to other standards, disciplines, or learner identity?

Principles of Minimalist Instructional Design

Minimalist instructional design requires establishing systems and structures in the classroom that help create more possibilities for learning while minimizing the work that keeps teachers from what really matters: building humanizing relationships with learners and helping every child grow. When systems and structures are sustainable, they allow teachers to be mindful and present in the most human components of teaching.

To design instruction with minimalism in mind, consider the following guiding principles:

- Use backward design (Wiggins & McTighe, 2005) for long-term planning.
- Look for connections between standards to teach multiple skills at once.
- Maintain minimalist documentation practices, such as journaling and portfolios.
- Choose deindustrialized, versatile, and rich learning tasks.
- Universally design learning tasks and the learning environment.
- Become an edtech minimalist.

Use Backward Design for Long-Term Planning

Teachers often wonder whether using backward design is sustainable; it seems like significantly more work than simply following a manual that has already been planned out. The problem is that curriculum manuals change, often mirroring change in high-level administrators, which contributes to initiative fatigue and creates unsustainable patterns that prevent teachers from honing their craft. Moreover, asking teachers to simply follow boxed curriculum promotes mindless teaching; when teachers do not have a manual to follow, or encounter challenges the manual hasn't anticipated, they are unsure how to proceed. As the preschool teacher from New York observed, "Every time we got a new instructional coordinator, a new administrator, a new chancellor, governor, [or] mayor, or a new buzzword became popular, teachers were expected to roll out the new agenda."

Backward design offers a solution. No matter what program teachers are expected to pull from, sound instructional design does not change. Leveraging backward design is more sustainable long-term, even if it feels like a bit more work up front. This is in part because different resources can be used for already designed units, but it is also because the process instills a way of thinking that will sustain planning and preparation throughout a teacher's career. This is not to say that schools should not provide teachers with foundational resources; sharing universally adopted materials and a common vision for teaching can support sustainability efforts. However, teachers should feel empowered to modify and shape these resources to meet students' needs.

Backward design creates a structure within which teachers can plan for instruction by clarifying desired results, identifying acceptable pieces of evidence, and creating a flexible learning plan that can act as a road map when things get messy. Teachers can even work foundational resources into their instructional design so that they do not have to start from scratch. (This also allows teachers to comply with district regulations requiring them to incorporate elements of boxed curricula or other foundational resources.) Because the structure of backward design also allows for flexibility, instruction can be both mindful and responsive to learners, easily adjusted to account for new data resulting from formative assessment.

Coaching teachers to follow curriculum manuals verbatim produces various negative consequences. Planning is mindless; teachers become reliant on the manual to know what to teach. Adjusting instruction as needs arise is challenging. Teachers struggle to pivot in the moment because they are not incentivized to think on their own. There are fewer opportunities for partnership with learners, as student contributions inevitably require a deviation from the manual. Finally, this

Committing to partnership with learners to teach sustainably requires breaking away from the teaching manual and promoting teacher autonomy to meet learners' needs.

maximalist approach sends the implicit message that teachers must "cover" the entirety of the manual. Backward design, in contrast, allows for more intentionality around what is being taught and why, helping teachers eliminate unnecessary activities and ensure that what they explore with learners is worth everyone's time.

In the Understanding by Design framework developed by Grant Wiggins and Jay McTighe (2005), Stage 1 of backward design is to identify desired results. This stage of the planning process allows teachers to not only determine what standards they must cover over the course of the year but also deconstruct those standards, find concomitance within standard sets, and even connect standards from one content area to standards from others (i.e., an embodied approach). This stage also provides a framework within which teachers can evaluate how lessons connect to learning outcomes. If the lesson or activity they want to include does not relate to Stage 1, it is not an intentional choice, and it should be cut from the unit.

In Stage 2, teachers create a robust assessment framework, within which they will collect evidence of student learning using sustainable documentation practices that consistently generate such evidence. Think of "evidence of learning" as a sustainable energy source in your classroom. Both teacher and learners can derive energy from harvesting evidence of learning, which informs instruction for teachers and self-reflection for learners. Backward design allows for intentional assessment planning, supporting long-term sustainability.

Stage 3 invites teachers to create a learning unit plan. It is important to shift toward minimalism here (see the sample unit plan in Appendix A). The learning unit plan should include (1) a reusable lesson structure that facilitates open-ended tasks, using the workshop model (Chapter 6 will address this model in detail), (2) options for documenting learning in partnership with learners (e.g., journals, portfolios), (3) a menu of choices for learners, and (4) arcs where open-ended tasks are grouped together and paired with learning menu options.

For the learning unit plan to be successful and sustainable, you must do the following:

- Consider learner identity (see Chapter 1) and current levels of proficiency with regard to academic outcomes.
- Build productive classroom routines and agreements that help learners operate with agency (see Chapters 2 and 3).

- Leverage sustainable, process-oriented assessment practices (see Chapter 5).
- Feel empowered to respond to student learning, adjusting instruction and task order as you gather more data about student learning (see Chapter 6).
- Start the planning process far in advance of instruction.

At first, backward design might feel challenging, but this does not mean it is unsustainable. Practices are sustainable when they become easier over time, leveraging ritual and experience to do so. That said, it takes some experience to become comfortable with the practice, so don't try to make it perfect the first time around. You may also want to wean yourself from boxed curriculum, implementing backward design in only a few units to start. However, if you begin planning for the next unit far enough in advance, you will see that both the preparation itself and the *process* of designing with the end in mind makes your teaching more flexible, responsive, and sustainable.

Look for Connections Between Standards

A high school teacher from Illinois shared that state and national standards create the situation of "teaching to a test and . . . take the fun out of education." Teachers cannot change the fact that their lessons must align with education standards, but they can change *how* they align them. Taking an embodied approach to teaching standards by looking for concomitance—natural connections—can address this challenge and simplify planning, preparation, and teaching. Standards that connect to one another can be taught and assessed together. Using backward design, particularly Stages 1 and 2, often reveals these connections.

For example, consider a set of 3rd grade math standards related to area:

CCSS.3.MD.5. Recognize area as an attribute of plane figures and understand concepts of area measurement.

a. A square with side length 1 unit, called "a unit square," is said to have "one square unit" of area, and can be used to measure area.

b. A plane figure which can be covered without gaps or overlaps by n unit squares is said to have an area of n square units.

CCSS.3.MD.6. Measure areas by counting unit squares (square cm, square m, square in, square ft, and improvised units).

CCSS.3.MD.7. Relate area to the operations of multiplication and addition.

a. Find the area of a rectangle with whole-number side lengths by tiling it, and show that the area is the same as would be found by multiplying the side lengths.

b. Multiply side lengths to find areas of rectangles with whole-number side lengths in the context of solving real-world and mathematical problems, and represent whole-number products as rectangular areas in mathematical reasoning.

c. Use tiling to show in a concrete case that the area of a rectangle with whole-number side lengths a and $b + c$ is the sum of $a \times b$ and $a \times c$. Use area models to represent the distributive property in mathematical reasoning.

d. Recognize area as additive. Find areas of rectilinear figures by decomposing them into nonoverlapping rectangles and adding the areas of the nonoverlapping parts, applying this technique to solve real-world problems. (National Governors Association Center for Best Practices & Council of Chief State School Officers, 2010, p. 25)

Each of these standards relates to the same skill: calculating the area of rectilinear figures. It is generally safe to assume that students who can calculate the area of a given figure using the standard algorithm (i.e., multiplying base times height) will likely be able to calculate the area by counting squares. Your tool for students to self-assess their mastery of the standard could be a proficiency scale (Marzano, 2009), a single-point rubric (Dietz, 2000), or a graduated rubric.

A proficiency-scale rubric (see Figure 4.1) deconstructs the 3rd grade standard and accounts for varying levels of proficiency. Whereas Levels 0 to 2

FIGURE 4.1

Proficiency-Scale Rubric

	Proficiency	Feedback
4	I can calculate the area of triangles and parallelograms.	
3*	I can calculate the area of rectilinear shapes using multiplication.	
2	I can calculate the area of rectilinear shapes by skip-counting rows or columns of squares.	
1	I can calculate the area of rectilinear shapes by counting unit squares.	
0	With help, I can calculate the area of rectilinear shapes by counting unit squares.	

*Indicates grade-level expectation.

anticipate what progressing toward proficiency might look like, Level 4 incorporates an enrichment learning objective. Note that numbering levels can be misleading, as learning progress is not actually linear. Also note that, in addition to spanning several standards, this rubric's addition of a Level 4 learning objective can complicate things: if a skill is present on the rubric, you must provide explicit tasks to assess it. Some might characterize Level 4 as "going above and beyond," but if the criteria are not explicitly articulated and assessed, the objective becomes subjective, inequitable, and unsustainable.

A single-point rubric (see Figure 4.2) lists success criteria in the middle. This type of rubric can be used by both students and teachers, with learners simply checking off criteria to show mastery and teachers providing details on qualitative strengths and challenges related to each criterion. For instance, if a child can calculate area only by counting squares, the teacher might make a note in the Challenges column while still giving credit for calculating the area. For a child who demonstrates mastery (i.e., both criteria checked off), the teacher might add another challenge (e.g., "I wonder if you can figure out how to calculate the area of triangles") in the Challenges column.

FIGURE 4.2

Single-Point Rubric

Strengths	Success Criteria	Challenges
	I can calculate the area of rectilinear shapes.	
	I can differentiate between measuring in length and measuring in area.	

Some teachers prefer a graduated rubric (see Figure 4.3), which provides a structure for learners to self-assess where they are in relation to meeting the grade-level standard. This can be especially helpful as a positive framing for learners who might have nothing to check off on a single-point rubric. The gradation still offers functional improvement through simplicity; "not yet" or "starting to" can look different for different kids. The open-ended feedback section allows learners to describe why they feel they are at the stage they are and gives teachers space to provide responsive feedback.

It is also helpful to look for concomitance—connections—across subject areas. One year, my team and I rewrote an interdisciplinary unit related to the American Revolutionary War, a common topic for students in 5th grade. Instead of writing three separate units for reading, writing, and social studies,

FIGURE 4.3

Graduated Rubric

Learning Goal	Not Yet	Starting To	Got It!	Feedback
I can calculate the area of rectilinear shapes.	☐	☐	☐	
I can differentiate between measuring in length and measuring in area.	☐	☐	☐	

we wrote one unit on human values, with the essential question *When does someone decide it's time to make a change?* Instruction for the unit incorporated the following activities:

- In reading, we explored historical fiction, with explicit instruction in literature standards related to character, setting, and figurative language.
- In writing, learners created newspapers, recounting historical events and figures, with explicit instruction in informational text standards related to citing text evidence, comparing text structures, and synthesizing information.
- In social studies, we explored standards related to history and geography, analyzing causes and effects of various historical events.

This interdisciplinary learning felt embodied, intentional, and more sustainable: we targeted clearly defined desired results and implemented performance tasks and assessments connected to the standards we were teaching. The plan empowered us to be flexible with our instruction, gradually supporting learners toward our collective end goals.

Maintain Minimalist Documentation Practices

Stage 2 of backward design invites teachers to consider how they will collect evidence of student learning—an energy source for the classroom. Evidence of student learning is like the fruits of your labor: you harvest it in order to figure out where to go next. My friend and colleague John Almarode would refer to this as a consistent "generation of evidence" (France & Almarode, 2022).

To keep from being overwhelmed, teachers must be intentional with what they deem acceptable evidence of student learning while taking an embodied approach to evidence generation. Both teachers and learners must be able to see connections between learning artifacts and instruction to tell the rich story of a child's learning journey. Following are some suggestions to sustainably support the practice of evidence generation.

Identify "containers" for learning artifacts. For me, these containers are portfolios and journals, in which every student learning artifact can be found. Portfolios allow for an embodied approach to assessing learning. Instead of evaluating learning artifacts individually, students' learning journeys can be understood using multiple pieces of evidence. Although I recommend offering students choice regarding which artifacts they include in their portfolios, you will also want them to include certain required elements. Both types of artifacts will aid learners in telling the story of their learning over the course of the year.

When I taught at the elementary school level, my students maintained three journals: a "thinking" journal, a math journal, and a writing journal. All learning artifacts related to independent reading, social studies, or reading workshop went into their thinking journals. All tasks related to math went into the math journal. All drafts of writing projects were contained in the writing journal.

Each of these journals told a single, embodied story of the learner's journey. Because journaling was an almost daily practice in all subjects, my students could easily look back over days or weeks to reflect on how they had grown. The journals offered me both an opportunity to reflect on my students' growth and insight into areas where they might be stagnating. Because everything was housed in their journals and portfolios—and because learners were partners in organizing and maintaining these containers of evidence—I did not have to manage a file cabinet of learning artifacts. I also wasn't grading, scoring, and returning meaningless assignments, sending them home to be recycled or lost. The use of student journals leads to an overall reduction of industrialized, worksheet-based resources that generally look more like busywork than fruitful learning.

> Making learners partners in the process of assessment becomes sustainable through shared responsibility.

When identifying projects or assignments, I would ask myself, *How is this learning artifact going to help each child tell the story of their learning?* If I could not answer that question, it probably wasn't worth assigning or recording in the journals and portfolios.

Build rubrics with clear success criteria that can be used over the course of an entire unit. If you are planning for student learning in an embodied and intentional way, the rubrics you create in Stage 2 of backward design (whether proficiency based, single point, or graduated) should be usable for all learning tasks over the course of a unit. Imagine eliminating the need for identifying point totals for individual assignments! Such point totals are often unhelpful for both teachers and learners; they neither describe the story of learning nor provide learners actionable steps. Rubrics help learners reflect on their areas of strength and challenge and help teachers draw connections between learning tasks, enabling planning in *arcs*. Arc-style planning—which is discussed further in Chapter 6—allows planning in longer chunks of time, finding connections between learning tasks to gradually build knowledge. Using the same overarching rubric also ensures that you are intentional regarding content presented to learners and the types of artifacts you assess. If it doesn't relate to the rubric, then it might not be worth collecting, assessing, and reflecting on.

Reduce reliance on worksheet- and workbook-based pedagogies. Workbook- and worksheet-based pedagogies require students to answer relatively closed-ended questions, filling in boxes or lines for the purpose of finding a single correct answer. These types of learning artifacts are less helpful in truly understanding who learners are and how they are thinking than portfolios and journals are. They are focused on the *product* of learning rather than the *process*. It is more sustainable to take a process-driven approach to assessment and documentation, which more effectively helps learners tell the story of their growth.

In some cases, the average worksheet or workbook page includes as many as 20 to 30 problems for students to complete and teachers to grade and assess. Journaling, on the other hand, requires a single rich, open-ended, learner-driven task for each lesson. This is minimalist for obvious reasons: one task to review is much less work to review than 20 to 30 problems on a worksheet. But using open-ended tasks such as journaling is also more intentional: they make a students' processes visible so that teachers learn much more about how students are thinking and where their misconceptions might lie.

Create an assessment calendar for each unit. During Stage 2 of backward design, teachers develop evaluative criteria that can be used over the entire course of the unit, as well as performance tasks and other evidence that will provide insight into the success criteria. The next step is to decide when you will conduct these formal performance tasks.

Although every learning task allows for informal assessment and feedback, I tend to schedule one independent task to be collected and formally assessed, from once per week at most to once every two weeks at minimum. I usually schedule these formal assessments at the end of a sequence of learning tasks from one arc that feels related to another (see, e.g., the sample unit plan in Appendix A; Arc 1 focuses on counting collections).

At the end of a learning arc, students should independently complete a formal assessment task that provides information on each individual learner and informs instruction for the following arc. Although other tasks throughout a unit may be supported by you or other students, scheduling a formal assessment task to be completed independently provides insight into what learners can accomplish on their own. Formal assessment tasks for succeeding arcs incorporate learning from preceding units and employ similar tasks (e.g., the learning menus referenced in Chapter 6 and in the sample plan in Appendix A).

Setting up a calendar to schedule formal assessment tasks allows the learning in between to be messy. Learning tasks from individual lessons need not be completed in their entirety, as long as fruitful learning results from each task, saving teachers time spent tracking learners down for missed or incomplete assignments. Thus, the purpose behind each learning task shifts: it is not about finding correct answers but rather geared toward uncovering new learning each day so that students gradually progress toward proficiency on the formal assessment tasks in the assessment calendar. A calendar of formal assessment also enables flexibility. Teachers can change the order of learning tasks or even insert new ones in response to student needs to support progress toward the formal assessment. Ultimately, you will formally assess roughly four to six learning artifacts per unit, rather than every activity learners complete on a daily basis.

Choose Deindustrialized, Versatile, and Rich Learning Tasks

Often, worksheets contain many items because the learning tasks are rather shallow, leading some learners to move through problems quickly and mindlessly. As an alternative to numerous shallow tasks that create more busywork, choose a single rich, deep, versatile learning task that requires learners to share in the demands of learning.

Counting collections activities are one example of a rich and versatile task. Counting collections require learners to count groups of objects in different ways. In the primary years, counting collections build flexibility and fluency with early numeracy skills, paving the way for efficient calculation (Franke et al., 2018). Learners can count one collection of objects in different ways, documenting each method in their math journals using a mixture of pictures, words, and equations. They can count by 1s or skip-count by any number they choose; they can arrange the objects in rows, arrays, 5-frames, or 10-frames. Counting collections offer many possibilities for learning and, no matter the learner, options for sustained engagement in the task throughout the entirety of the learning block. (Chapter 6 further addresses this type of sustained engagement.)

Universally Design Learning Tasks and the Learning Environment

Rich and versatile learning tasks are more sustainable when they are universally designed, that is, designed with all learners in mind (CAST, 2018). Unsustainable and misguided approaches to personalized learning or differentiated instruction encourage teachers to create different tasks for different groups of learners—high-, medium-, and low-level lessons; individualized playlists of activities; and web-based adaptive programs that automate content based on level.

Universally designing tasks liberates teachers from creating multiple tasks and monitoring them for different groups and allows for meeting all learners' needs. In designing the task, however, you must be intentional, ensuring that it has access points for all learners. You need to take an embodied approach to *facilitating* the task, helping learners see connections between themselves and their peers and appreciate the diversity of methods and responses.

Again, counting collections provides a good example. The task in the sample unit plan in Appendix A is universally designed; it incorporates varied access points. Some learners will need to count by 1s to start, perhaps using printed grid paper, 5-frames, or 10-frames to scaffold the structuring of their counting. Other students will be able to flexibly count in a variety of ways. Some might even be ready to pair their counting strategies with expressions and number sentences. Although it is up to students to choose a strategy or method that works for them, the teacher circulates around the room, asking insightful questions or providing ideas about what students might try to make their methods for counting more efficient, or perhaps connecting their methods to addition or multiplication.

Rich learning tasks require partnering with learners. Learners must use their agency to make choices about methods to use, and they must exhibit sustained engagement with the task. A learning environment where students are empowered to make choices on their own contributes to sustainable teaching. Because students are doing more in terms of making choices, teachers will have to relinquish some of the control they have over learning in the classroom, a courageous and vulnerable move.

The learning environment, too, must be universally designed. If you anticipate that some learners will need grid paper, 5-frames, or 10-frames to assist them in counting, those materials must be readily available. Similarly, if you know that some learners will need sensory breaks to maintain consistent regulation during the school day, you must dedicate an area in the room for this. (Chapter 6 further explores organizing and maintaining rich resource libraries in classrooms.)

> Partnering with learners and letting them choose their own path requires a high tolerance for uncertainty while teaching.

Become an Edtech Minimalist

It seems like there is a technology tool for almost everything. When I first started using one-to-one devices in my classroom, I made the mistake of downloading too many applications for different content areas. It is important to keep in mind that educational technology—often referred to as edtech—in the classroom should serve specific purposes (France, 2020, 2022; Puentedura, 2015):

- Minimize complexity.
- Maximize individual power and potential.
- Reimagine learning.
- Preserve or enhance human connection.

Using web-based, adaptive technologies that send content to learners at their levels is not sustainable in the long term. This type of technology is disempowering, industrialized, and inequitable. Moreover, it chips away at human connection, beckoning learners toward screens for gamified instruction (e.g., Kahoot) rather than toward their peers for humanizing relationships grounded in learning. These programs seem effective when they are new and exciting, but it does not take long for tools like these to lose their luster. They quickly become just another mechanism for industrializing learning through right and wrong answers, layered with competition and further marginalizing our most vulnerable learners. To be edtech minimalists, teachers must ensure that the technology they choose streamlines learning, creates access points for all learners, and makes their lives less complicated, not more.

When choosing technology, consider tools that make documenting learning easier. For instance, you may want to create digital portfolios using Seesaw or Google Drive to make it easier for students to manage learning artifacts and share them with their families electronically. Or you might want tools that offer possibilities for learners to demonstrate learning. Electronic math manipulatives or concept-mapping tools like Popplet create avenues for learners to show their thinking in a variety of ways. Tools like Google Docs increase opportunities for collaboration and enhance learner agency.

My shift to edtech minimalism happened when I realized that I was doing a lot to serve the technology we were using, and it was doing little to serve me. To this day, I only use tech tools when I feel like they are streamlining learning and providing more access to learners in my classroom.

Implications for Professional Learning

Professional learning that is not streamlined generates problems related to initiative fatigue. It is important to remember that trying to change everything at once will not only overload teachers but is also a deficit-framing approach to professional learning. Instead, build on teachers' current gifts, find clarity on goals, and prioritize incremental shifts in practice that will in time contribute to broad-scale shifts in pedagogy.

Personalized professional learning does not have to mean individualizing professional curriculum for teachers. Instead, it entails thinking of personalized learning in three dimensions (France, 2019): (1) shaping the collective consciousness of the school, (2) aligning team-based goals to collective goals, and (3) leveraging coaching models to engender incremental shifts in practice that will move the entire school toward collective goals. Taking a minimalist approach to professional learning goals streamlines professional learning, making it intentional and embodied.

Shaping the collective consciousness requires having a clear vision; setting reasonable, time-bound goals for the school year; and establishing clear expectations for quality teaching, preferably using a high-quality teaching framework. These structures will support personalized professional learning in the second and third dimensions.

To create team-based goals related to the school vision and schoolwide goals, coaches or administrative teams should consult with teams to build clear, actionable, and time-bound goals related to problems of practice or specific wonderings within the classroom. For example, if the school has set a schoolwide goal around using backward design to plan units of instruction, it may be logical for different grade levels to identify different goals related to this process. Perhaps one team can focus on deconstructing standards in Stage 1, while another team sets a goal around creating rich performance tasks in Stage 2. This approach is sustainable both because it is embodied and intentional, and because it creates space for individual teams to exercise their agency.

The third dimension of personalization allows for a healthy amount of individualism. In order to preserve connectedness to the collective, teachers should set goals related to the collective goals of the school. This allows for connectedness between teacher–learners, as well as sustainability for coaches and administrators, because all goals are related to one another.

Coaching on the individual level also enables incremental shifts in practice. Monumental shifts in practice are not sustainable. Remember, learning occurs within the zone of proximal development. Coaches need to meet teachers where they are, acknowledge their gifts, and use inquiry to support them in professional growth. Pushing teachers into changing too much too quickly results in burnout, partly because it is hard to feel a sense of mastery in the face of too much change all at once. Also, teachers already have a lot of work to do. Focusing on small shifts that can be implemented gradually throughout the year sustains their energy reserves.

Jim Knight's (2018) Impact Cycle is one minimalist structure for coaching. It is intentional—it drives teachers toward action—and creates a sustainable ritual for professional learning that can be executed with repetition over the course of the year. This ritualistic cycle of inquiry and reflection creates a pattern of thinking within teachers that allows them to express curiosity about

 Professional learning rituals like coaching create a sense of consistency, allowing for learning to gradually emerge through repetitive cycles over the course of a year.

their practice, gain insight into the clear picture of current reality, and identify specific action steps to improve their practice.

Something's Gotta Give

In *De-Implementation: Creating the Space to Focus on What Works,* Peter DeWitt (2022) advocates for cutting out low-impact practices in schools to make space for high-value practices that benefit students. Justin Reich, director of the MIT Teaching Systems Lab, describes this tactic as "subtraction in action" (2022, para. 7).

Subtracting unsustainable practices can be liberating, encouraging teachers to be minimalist by taking some things off their plates—and simultaneously making room for sustainable practices that deepen learning. Embracing minimalist instructional design makes it easier to assess and respond to learners in a sustainable manner. Because there are fewer fires to put out, there is more time to respond to learners in an intentional manner based on the result of formative assessments. The next two chapters explore process-driven assessment and responsive instruction as pathways to even greater sustainability, using minimalism as a foundation.

Chapter Summary

Minimalist learning design streamlines planning and preparation for instruction. This approach requires being intentional about learning task design and ensuring that units are embodied—which in turn entails finding concomitance among standards and examining how learning tasks are related to one another, gradually building knowledge and skills. Streamlining planning and preparation also requires universally designing learning tasks and the learning environment. These steps reduce teacher workload while encouraging partnership with learners, providing them with choices about how they interact with rich tasks in their journals. For teaching to be sustainable, teachers must embrace learning as a process, unique to each child and driven by student choices.

STOP AND REFLECT

Identify some action steps you can take to shift toward minimalist instructional design.

- **Amplify:** Which sustainable practices are you already implementing that you want to keep or increase?
- **Alter:** What do you want to change or stop entirely?
- **Activate:** Which new practices would you like to implement to work toward sustainability?

5

Process over Product

ESSENTIAL QUESTION: What's the story?

Early in my teaching career, I spent many nights sitting in my living room sorting piles of worksheets, activities, and "centers" that my students had completed during different learning blocks throughout the day. They would complete them, and I would assign them a point total; some students wouldn't turn things in, which led to me spending time chasing them down so they would. I would take points off for "late work," only to find that the grades I was giving my students were not reflective of what they could do in class.

It dawned on me, one of those evenings when I sat at home with my piles of papers, sipping my well-deserved glass of red wine, that I was missing work from at least one student for every activity. I looked at the papers, adorned with 8s, 9s, or 10s, and at my computer screen displaying a maze of boxes in a spreadsheet with cumulative point totals. *This isn't telling me anything about my students,* I thought. *It's all just serving the gradebook. None of it is serving us.*

I tossed all those papers into the recycling bin, and I never looked back.

Within weeks, I began exploring portfolio-based assessment, leveraging what I had learned about standards-based assessment and proficiency scales (Marzano, 2009; see Figure 4.1). My goal was for assessment to become more meaningful and learner-driven, rather than a mere compliance metric that created more busywork for both my students and me. In some ways, I met my goal. By using learner-friendly proficiency scales for student self-assessment, we managed to meet multiple sustainability needs:

- Assessment was more meaningful, with each number on the proficiency scale now connected to qualitative success criteria to help learners articulate their current proficiency.
- Assessment became a shared responsibility, as learners were assessing learning artifacts independently and reducing my workload.
- Assessment became humanized through learner agency, cultivating learners' self-awareness around academic outcomes.

To build a proficiency scale, you take a learning objective or standard and deconstruct it, describing what it might look like (with specificity) to exceed, meet, and approach expectations. Each descriptor is usually paired with a number from 0 to 4. The indicator at Level 3 summarizes a grade-level expectation. Level 4 represents something "above and beyond," whereas 0 to 2 represent gradations of approaching proficiency.

Although my proficiency scales were a step forward, they were neither perfect nor sustainable in the long term. The only efficient way to assess this many artifacts was to use the numbering system that the proficiency scales provided. At first, I was not aware of just how similar proficiency scales and the accompanying number system were to traditional grades. In far too many instances, I noticed learners seeking out a number rather than the feedback and reflection that I hoped would come as a result of using proficiency scales. In their eyes, a rating of 4 was not much different than getting an *A*. I had simply swapped out letters for numbers, with the slight functional improvement of pairing qualitative success criteria with the numbers (in hopes of enhancing reflection). Yet my students' and my reflections still focused on the *product* of learning, as opposed to the *process*.

Product-Focused Assessment Is Unsustainable

Assessment was a hot topic in the #SustainableTeaching Survey, with over one third of respondents describing current assessment practices as unsustainable, citing standardized assessment, a culture of control and fear around assessment, and the frequency and duration of assessment.

"Assessment is over the top," shared a 5th grade teacher from Ohio. "We calculated how much time we spend in diagnostic testing and state testing, and it added up to nine full days of instruction (about 45 hours)." Consider regular assessments such as i-Ready, DIBELS and DIBELS Maze, and Forefront Math; schools that use such assessments do this type of testing three times a year. With the average school year about 180 days long, some schools could spend approximately 15 percent of the school year engaged in testing—not including common formal assessment tasks or classroom-based summative assessments.

Emphasizing the product in assessment is unsustainable because it is grounded in the industrialization of schooling. This focus makes learners the *objects* of schooling, dehumanizing them and, in the worst cases, controlling their learning for the purpose of high standardized test scores. Learners should, instead, be the *subjects* of an ever-evolving narrative of learning. When they are, there is sustainability; learners partner with educators in the process of self-reflection. This is not to say that the product is irrelevant or meaningless; it simply means that process should take precedence over product. It is within the process of learning that we are able to tell the story of a child's learning journey. The most effective way to do this is to focus on the feedback learners receive while in our classrooms. Doing so meets learners where they are, providing them next steps as the story of their learning unfolds.

> When assessment is about capturing the learning process, we can partner with learners so their voices narrate the story of their journey.

Embracing the Process to Tell the Story of Learning

Respondents to the #SustainableTeaching survey identified assessment practices they felt lead to sustainable teaching: learner-driven assessment, assessing for growth, and going gradeless. But before considering specific practices for emphasizing process over product (as well as identifying sustainable assessment practices), we must first look at the way we think about assessment.

There needs to be a shift in thinking about assessment, from a focus on achievement toward a focus on competence. Assessment should not be teachers simply checking a box or students reaching a bar raised above their heads; it should help learners connect their efforts to their progress, making it visible to them. This shift makes teaching more sustainable, because when learners can connect their efforts to their progress, they are more likely to see that they can play a role in sustaining their own learning. In short, they see that their efforts will pay off.

Process-based assessment will not feel "efficient," especially when you are just beginning. Therefore, you must resist calls to accelerate learning and instead *decelerate* it. Emphasizing competence and granting permission for teachers to slow down creates space and time to reframe assessment as story-telling. In this way, teaching becomes sustainable and learning sustained—and more likely to be transferred into learners' long-term memory because the telling of the story adds meaning. Learners are more likely to retain a story that holds meaning, as opposed to a series of compliance tasks that label them as proficient or not proficient.

Competence

A high school teacher from Delaware described grading as a "vicious cycle":

I grade papers and enter grades. Students and families have no idea what those grades even mean. I get questions about the grades. I spend time playing "throw the policies out the window" and just letting kids make up work (which doesn't ever reflect what they've learned) just so that they don't fail. I hate the system, kids hate the system, parents hate the system, but we all do it because we feel we have to.

The system of grading and norm ranking was never intended to build competence in learners. Instead, it was built with the intention of ranking students for job placement. Learners with the highest rankings were seen as the most desirable candidates. These practices date back to the 1600s, when grades were first used at Ivy League schools. But even educators in schools that have begun to embrace standards-based or competency-based assessment face challenges, as students who want to pursue postsecondary education need transcripts with grades on them.

A focus on competence, however, is intrinsically motivating and therefore sustainable. When learners can connect their efforts to tangible progress, they are more likely to engage in school (Pink, 2009), share in the responsibility of sustaining learning, and feel a sense of competence.

The word *competence* comes from the Latin *petere,* meaning "to strive or seek." To have a sense of competence, then, does not mean meeting minimum expectations; it is, instead, a sense that one is capable—not only of meeting grade-level expectations but also of growing continuously and striving for deeper and richer levels of understanding within a standard, skill, or task.

Deceleration

Although the term *acceleration* is not new in the context of education, since 2021, it has been applied more broadly, posed as an alternative to *remediation* and other deficit-framing terms such as *learning loss*. And in many ways, the approaches encouraged by advocates of learning acceleration are in line with practices outlined in this book, from finding concomitance among standards to teach more efficiently, to making learning visible through process-oriented assessment (Almarode et al., 2021).

That said, it is hard to escape the connotation of the word "acceleration." Acceleration implies a speeding up of learning; it stands to reason that this push to increase learning speed is grounded in the notion that learning *needs* to speed up in the wake of the pandemic, given discrepancies in test scores from pre- and postpandemic eras. The reality is that asking teachers to speed learning up puts even more pressure on them to bear the responsibility of solving problems that reside outside their loci of control. Furthermore, asking teachers to accelerate learning in response to perceived *losses* in learning makes the term *learning acceleration* equally as deficit-framing as *learning loss*. After all, we wouldn't need to accelerate learning if it were not currently moving too slowly.

The clamor for accelerated learning brings into question the origin of the calls. One cannot help but see a connection between the desire to raise test scores and accelerating learning. Acceleration—at least nominally—offers schools a solution for closing the gap between how educators believe students *should be* performing on standardized assessments and how they *are* performing. This framing of learning is troubling, in part because it is a response to flawed standardized test metrics that dehumanize learners, but also because it demands students learn faster, when what they really need is to slow down, taking time to heal from a traumatic few years.

> Recovering from the COVID-19 pandemic should not entail accelerating gains in test scores; it should be about healing wounds, some of which were inflicted long before the pandemic began.

Campbell's Law describes the way standardized testing has influenced teaching and learning: "The more any quantitative social indicator is used for social decision-making, the more subject it will be to corruption pressures and the more apt it will be to distort and corrupt the social processes it is intended to monitor" (Campbell, 1979). Standardized testing has been distorting the process it has been intended to monitor for decades. Since its origins in the Reagan administration's report on the state of U.S. education, *A Nation at Risk* (National Commission on Excellence in Education, 1983), and evolving over the years in iterations such as America 2000, Goals 2000, the No Child Left Behind Act, and Race to the Top, it continues to distort teaching through an overemphasis on a *product* of learning.

Decelerating learning does not mean that students learn less, but rather that they are encouraged to pause so that they may learn in a way that is transferable. The process of self-reflection slows learning down, in a manner of speaking, but does so intentionally, so that students learn deeply, not quickly. By taking the time to reflect on learning—identifying strengths, challenges, and next steps in the learning process—students consolidate their learning, building a sense of competence, self-awareness, and metacognitive skills that will transfer to other areas of schooling. Such deep learning and consolidation of knowledge and skills can only be done if students are provided those quiet moments to reflect and consolidate learning. These pauses also allow for regeneration after engaging in the often taxing process of learning. Chapter 4 discussed the importance of minimalism in instructional design. When instructional plans are minimalist and leverage the fruits of learner agency, teachers are granted permission to slow down and let learners soak in meaningful learning experiences.

The same goes for professional learning. The drive to accelerate professional learning, particularly through plug-and-play programs or rigid step-by-step pedagogies, actually works against sustainability in the long run. Providing one-size-fits-all programs does not enable teachers to build conceptual knowledge or mindful practice; instead, it creates mindless teachers who struggle with how to respond when lessons take unexpected turns or learners respond in ways the curriculum did not anticipate.

 Slowing down allows energy reserves to regenerate so that deep, transferable learning can continue to happen.

STOP AND REFLECT

- Are you, in your classroom or school, already embracing process-driven approaches to assessment?
- In what ways is your approach to assessment grounded in compliance and accelerating learning to raise test scores?
- What steps have you taken to slow learning down, partnering with learners to help them tell their stories?

A Pedagogy for Process-Driven Assessment

The pedagogy for process-driven assessment includes a series of moves teachers make to partner with learners in the process of gauging what is working, what is not working, and what the next steps are. The following moves are a good start as you seek sustainability with assessment practices:

- Shift to standards-based assessment.
- Create rituals around goal setting and assessment.
- Anticipate learner responses.
- Embed assessment into the learning period.
- Limit corrective feedback.

Shift to Standards-Based Assessment

Results from the #SustainableTeaching survey did not reflect a consensus on the value (or lack thereof) of education standards. Some respondents considered "anything standardized" as unsustainable (because each student is different). Others, like David Frangiosa, high school science teacher and co-author of *Going Gradeless* (Burns & Frangiosa, 2021), suggested that transitioning to standards-driven, mastery learning proves more sustainable.

"In the gradeless model that we developed and have been implementing for the past few years, it has become very easy to identify where each student is in their learning journey and support them appropriately," he shared in the #SustainableTeaching survey. "There are no comparisons to other students. No ranking. No sorting. Students are met with strengths-based, descriptive feedback that coaches them to the next developmental level."

David also connected assessment with other mindset shifts explored in this book. He advocates for humanizing assessment practices, stating that "traditional grading [tends] to favor affluence, parental presence/support, and behaviors that skew toward white, Eurocentric values." Finally, he offered commentary on control- and compliance-driven practices, sharing that teachers must feel empowered to make shifts in grading practices. If administrators attempt to rigidly control grading practices, teachers will not be able to move toward more sustainable, humanizing forms of assessment.

At first glance, standards may not seem humanizing, but remember that standards provide a common language to clarify learning outcomes, ensuring equity for all students and clear success criteria for learners. That said, standard sets should be constantly revisited, revised, and reevaluated for bias. Often, it is not the standards themselves that create problems but rather how they are implemented. Standards can be implemented in sustainable and humanizing ways.

All 50 states have established "priority standards" that are most important for students to know and be able to do at different grade levels. In 2010, 46 states adopted the Common Core State Standards (CCSS), although since then, some of these states have repealed their use or developed a hybrid combining the CCSS with preexisting standards (World Population Review, n.d.). Chapter 4 described finding concomitance in standard sets and consolidating them in learner-friendly rubrics. All of these rubrics included space or opportunity for anecdotal feedback; you can tailor feedback in relation to standards, perhaps providing learners with suggestions for improvement or ways to challenge themselves to go deeper with their learning. Building rituals around standards-based assessment involves learners in the process of self-evaluation.

Create Assessment Rituals

There is sustainability in ritual; as rituals become familiar, they require less of a cognitive demand each time they are executed. Creating rituals for assessment requires identifying both flexible tools and a regular schedule with which to assess student learning. Following

 By finding assessment rituals that kids can use on their own, teaching becomes more sustainable because learners do not need teachers to support self-assessment and self-reflection.

are some examples of assessment rituals you can use in your classroom to promote sustainability.

Pre- and post-assessments (unit-based). Planning pre- and post-assessment is part of Stage 2 of backward design (Wiggins & McTighe, 2005; see Chapter 4). Pre-assessments offer teachers an opportunity to see what learners are bringing into a unit of study; they also give learners a chance to preview the unit's content, cultivating awareness around the assets they are bringing into the unit that might support them in overcoming obstacles in the new unit.

Many teachers responding to the #SustainableTeaching survey were concerned about the amount of assessment during the typical school year. But pre-assessment does not have to be intrusive. Consider the following examples:

- Design an open-ended task that incorporates essential success criteria. Have learners grapple with the task and take notes on what strategies they use conquer the task. Take note, too, of skills they need to complete the task. In this way, you can use a pre-assessment task for both student learning and assessment.
- Preview a learner-friendly rubric with students. They can rate themselves on the rubric, identifying words from the rubric they don't know. Ask students who feel they have already mastered the skills to create tasks they think would meet the success criteria.
- For writing projects, have learners make "flash drafts" from a prompt that relates to the success criteria. Flash drafts that consolidate all of a students' ideas on a topic provide insight into writing fluency, structure, and genre, even if students do not complete a draft in the time allotted.

Pre-assessment serves two functions. First, it provides initial information for both teacher and learners. This information is critical to decision making in future lessons. Second, it provides a point of comparison for later in the unit (i.e., post-assessment): learners can see how much they have grown. Process-driven assessment is sustainable because it aids learners in telling their own story, using multiple learning artifacts.

Reviewing evidence that was generated earlier in the learning sequence provides a tangible means for describing growth; learners will be able to point to two distinct pieces of evidence, measuring the same success criteria, from two distinct moments in time. This means post-assessment gets reframed, as well. Post-assessment is not about ensuring mastery on all standards (though that is the ultimate hope), as we know learners grow at different rates; instead, it is a way to celebrate growth since the pre-assessment.

Formal assessment tasks (weekly). Chapter 4 discussed creating a calendar that includes formal assessment tasks. Scheduling these every one to two weeks within an instructional unit allows both learners and teacher to obtain evidence of learning, aiding in reflection and the identification of next steps for learning.

Formally assessing once every one to two weeks also prevents grading from piling up, meaning that teachers can prioritize returning assessments to students with expediency, shortening feedback loops as much as possible. In fact, teachers might even consider guiding learners through a self-assessment in the classroom immediately after the formal assessment task, to make things more efficient and partner with learners in the process. If time does not permit that, teachers can assess students on their own and lead learners through a reflection ritual the following day, having them identify strengths, challenges, and next steps for learning, continuing the momentum already built in the unit. This also means that learning tasks or assignments that take place between formal assessments do not need to be formally assessed. Teachers can instead offer anecdotal, in-person feedback, guiding students gradually toward the next formal assessment.

 When learners are partners in the process of assessment, the energy demands of learning are distributed equitably between teacher and learners while making learners' experience richer and more meaningful.

Journal-based self-reflection. Journaling—discussed further in Chapter 6—supports sustainable assessment, flexible and responsive instruction, and minimalist instructional design. By having students regularly engage in journaling (in any subject), teachers create rituals around assessment—for both teacher (reflecting on student work in a grade-level team meeting or professional learning community) and students (via feedback in the journal). Journals also support flexible grouping, as teachers can pull groups based on the results of reviewing journals, even if it means reviewing strengths and challenges within journals in heterogeneous groups.

Journals also offer opportunities for learner-driven reflection; consider using them with students at the end of each learning block. Reflections help students tell the story of their learning, as opposed to simply measuring success in terms of correctness. Prompts for reflections can be open-ended or targeted toward a learning objective (see Figure 5.1 for examples).

FIGURE 5.1

Journal Prompts

Open-Ended	Targeted
• Today, I learned . . . • I am still puzzled by . . . • I discovered . . . • I used to . . . , but now I . . . • Next time, I will . . .	• Write what you learned today about determining the theme of a story. What are you still wondering about? • What is still puzzling you about multiplying fractions? What errors did you make today?

The prompt matters less than the ritual itself. What matters most is that kids get into the habit of doing this daily so that they are consistently reflecting on their successes and challenges and setting intentions or goals for the following day. At first, learners may not be sure what to write; model examples of reflections, providing sentence starters as an added scaffold. Some learners may need to share their reflections verbally before writing them down. Don't be surprised if they borrow your language at first—in fact, doing so is part of the learning process for developing the skill and vocabulary needed to self-assess. With time, they will be able to come up with more unique reflections.

Portfolio reflections. Portfolios offer ample opportunities for sustainable assessment. First, they act as a container for artifacts of learning. The most apparent of these artifacts are pre- and post-assessments and other formal assessment tasks you offer students along the way. Collecting these assessments in one place not only reduces your need to keep an organized file cabinet but also empowers learners to organize their own learning artifacts, providing a sense of ownership and building agency.

Portfolios can also serve as a container for artifacts learners choose to collect. Perhaps they wrote a draft in writing workshop or drew a picture of which they were especially proud. These works have a place in portfolios, as well, as they are part of the student's learning journey over the course of a year. Although digital portfolios are also an option, younger students often find it easier to page through paper portfolios to locate old artifacts, especially if they are organized by subject area and dated appropriately.

A word of caution: it is very important that teachers establish boundaries surrounding the content of learner portfolios. It is neither sustainable nor logical to archive every learning artifact. Portfolios fill up quickly if items are not selected with prudence, and too many artifacts dilute reflection and make the most meaningful ones hard to find.

I like the class to pull out their portfolios three to four times per year to engage in general reflection. During this time, learners are invited to look through their portfolios and focus on any area of learning they would like. Although you might keep the conversation open-ended, you may want to provide some structure to the reflection to scaffold the process, especially if it is new to learners. Here is one example:

1. Ask learners to spend five minutes silently exploring. Tell them they will have a chance to share with neighbors, but that you want them to spend five minutes noticing anything that piques their interest or pops out to them.

2. Next, have them turn to neighbors and share what they noticed. You can provide sentence stems like, "I noticed that . . ." or "This artifact popped out to me because . . . ."

3. Then, have them choose two artifacts to compare. If students struggle to choose two, have them choose a subject first. Then prompt them to choose something that shows how they have changed. "Look for something that shows what you used to do," I say, "and then find something that shows what you can do now."

4. What comes next is up to you. You could have students do a formal written reflection in their journal using some of the prompts from the journal reflections. You could also do a visual reflection, where learners tape or glue the two artifacts next to each other, writing "I used to . . ." and "Now I . . ." above each artifact. This alternative is especially powerful for younger learners or learners who are still learning to reflect using specific words.

Verbal closing reflections. Written reflection doesn't work for all kids. Do not force students for whom writing creates a barrier to only reflect in their journals. In fact, verbal reflection might be an appropriate scaffold to support students in eventually documenting their reflections in journals or portfolios.

Verbal closing reflections are an excellent substitute for formally documented reflections. They can be done individually, in small groups, or with the whole class. In fact, when facilitated with the whole class, learners gain exposure to all sorts of reflections, expanding their vocabulary for reflection as the year goes on.

All reflection formats follow a relatively simple structure: identify strengths or successes, generate challenges or questions, and determine next

steps. The simplest verbal ritual entails
three questions:

- What worked?
- What didn't work?
- What's next?

Keeping this ritual simple and streamlined increases the likelihood of build-

> Simplifying reflection makes it (✓) easier for learners to do it independently, creating replicable rituals that require little additional teacher energy.

ing new ways of thinking and being within learners. The hope is that self-
reflection will become a sustainable habit that transfers to other areas of
their lives.

Peer-to-peer feedback. Process-oriented assessment becomes more
sustainable when learners partner in the responsibility of providing feedback.
In peer-to-peer feedback, learners share in the energy demands of learning,
carrying some of the load of evaluating evidence of student learning. For this
tactic to be successful and productive, however, learners need to be taught
structures for giving and receiving feedback.

Starting with a learner-friendly rubric is critical. When building a ritual
around peer feedback, learners should be instructed to start by grounding
their feedback in the rubric. Eventually, you will empower them to provide
feedback outside of the rubric, but starting with the rubric raises the likelihood that the feedback will lead to progress in grade-level standards.

"Two stars and a wish" is one structure for providing feedback. "Two
stars" refers to two compliments, and the "wish" refers to corrective feedback.
You may want to prepare sentence frames (see Figure 5.2) for learners to get
them started.

Whatever structure you choose to use, ensure that there is space for both
praise and corrective feedback. You might also consider inviting learners
to build the list of sentence starters with you, using their language to fill an

---

FIGURE 5.2

Two Stars and a Wish

Stars Language	Wish Language
• I liked how . . . • _____ was effective because . . . • I think this meets expectations because . . . • I think this exceeds expectations because . . .	• Write what you learned today about determining the theme of a story. What are you still wondering about? • What is still puzzling you about multiplying fractions? What errors did you make today?

anchor chart. Contributing to the process increases the likelihood that students will be invested in it—and this process becomes another tool for telling the story of their learning journeys.

Scaffolded decision making. Assessment cannot and should not be something that is *done to* kids in a sustainable classroom. Instead, assessment should be a process in which teachers *engage with* learners, slowly building their agency over time.

"The learner needs to be the one who makes decisions about their progress," shared a middle school teacher from Iowa in the #Sustainable-Teaching survey. "Having a guiding adult is important, but the learner's own self-assessment is the only way that assessment can be real, impactful, and lasting."

The challenge here is that students need to learn how to make these choices, and teachers must be ready to host discussions, provide scaffolds, and identify tools that will support them. One option to help learners make assessment choices is a learning menu (Figure 5.3), which provides visual cues for students. The example in Figure 5.3 offers three choices for a math activity.

It is important to model for students how to choose from a learning menu. You might do a think-aloud, verbalizing the process for them:

- "I am working on skip-counting, so I'm going to choose the counting collection."

FIGURE 5.3

Learning Menu

After menu choices have been modeled for students and they are able to complete the activities independently, you can use graphic images to represent the activities on a chart, as in the example below.

Today's Menu: Make a choice that's right for you!		
Counting Collections	**What's Behind My Back?**	**Number Grid Puzzles**

Note: Counting Collections entails learners counting groups of objects in different ways, building fluency and flexibility with counting (Franke et al., 2018). For What's Behind My Back? one partner breaks a stick of counting cubes into two parts and the other must discern the value of the part that's behind their partner's back. Number Grid Puzzles asks learners to draw on number patterns to reassemble a 100s chart that is broken into pieces.

- "I want more practice with making 10s and 20s, so I'm going to play What's Behind My Back?"
- "I'm looking for a new challenge, so I'm going to try the number grid puzzles that we saw in morning meeting today."

You may want to have students write their names under their choice on a board so you can collect data on learners' choices. It's OK, too, if students don't pick what you consider to be the "correct" choice the first time around. During the workshop, you can adjust learner choices or give them feedback on which choice would be most appropriate for them. If they end up working on a choice that is less rigorous than you would like it to be, rest easy knowing that building fluency in any of these skills is productive, educative, and perfectly appropriate. You can always encourage learners to make a different choice the following day, if necessary.

Learning menus provide multiple sustainability benefits. First, they place boundaries around choice. Boundaries are necessary for learners of all ages, ensuring that their choices are productive and educative. Second, the boundaries allow teachers to be intentional with setting up choices, ensuring they align with the desired results of the unit plan. Finally, boundaries simplify learning, allowing teachers to limit unnecessary complexity.

Teaching learners to choose from learning menus builds learner agency while simplifying the potential complexity of providing learners choice in the classroom.

Anticipate Learner Responses

Going through the process of identifying learning goals, deconstructing standards, and creating standards-based rubrics prepares teachers to anticipate learner responses in the classroom. Anticipating learner responses directs focus on the different ways in which learners will interact with the curriculum. Preparing for these varied methods means ensuring that you have the proper scaffolds, tools, and strategies ready to support all learners.

I first learned about anticipating responses from my former colleague, Meghan Smith, now a PhD candidate at Stanford University, who also introduced me to using a T-chart to work through the process (see Figure 5.4; note that the Tyrone's Flowers task also fits into the sample unit plan in Appendix A).

FIGURE 5.4

Anticipating Student Responses

Task: Tyrone's Flowers

Tyrone is making bouquets of flowers. Each bouquet will have 5 flowers in it. He has both red and purple flowers to choose from. He wants all the bouquets to be different. Some will be entirely red. Some will be entirely purple. Others will be mixed.

How many different mixtures of red and purple flowers can Tyrone make?

Standard: This task addresses K.OA.A.3, a prerequisite skill for adding and subtracting efficiently within 20.

Student Response	Teacher Support
Learners are unsure where to begin.	Ask: *Which tools might help you show what the problem is asking?* If learners don't know what tools are available, provide a choice between drawing a picture or using a concrete manipulative like snap cubes.
Learners use a concrete manipulative (e.g., blocks, snap cubes, counters) to represent flowers.	Ask: *How might you show what you are doing in your math journal?*
Learners draw a picture in their math journal consisting of colored dots.	Ask: *How might you represent your model using numbers or equations?*
Learners draw a picture in the math journal, but it is either not colored or somewhat disorganized.	Ask: *How might you make your math model clearer to someone else?*
Learners write a series of equations (e.g., 1 + 4, 5 + 0), but the series is not in any type of order.	Ask: *How might you make this more organized? Could you make a second version that shows a pattern?*
Learners write a series of equations in order (e.g., 0 + 5, 1 + 4, 2 + 3).	Ask: *Are there any more possibilities? How can you prove to me there are no more possibilities?*
Learners write all equations for decomposing 5 (e.g., 0 + 5, 1 + 4, 2 + 3, 3 + 2, 4 + 1, 5 + 0).	Ask: *How can you prove to me there are no more possibilities? Will you explain this thinking?*
Learners quickly and easily do the task.	Offer enrichment: *What would this look like if Tyrone had 6 flowers per bouquet? 7? 8?* Offer an option (to build fluency and independence with other skills): *Would you like to select another choice from the learning menu?*

Anticipating learner responses benefits learners because it allows for varied learning pathways and processes while also connecting the entire class through a common, open-ended task. The benefit for teachers comes from not having to create different activities for different groups of learners. Instead, you differentiate in the moment based on the ways learners respond to the open-ended task.

This example demonstrates how minimalist instruction design and an open-ended task can support teachers in process-driven assessment. Process-driven assessment is less about getting a correct answer and more about meeting learners where they are, enriching the methods they choose, and gradually inching them toward greater efficiency and deeper understanding of concepts. It is true that, in some cases, correctness matters—but in many other cases, what is more important is what learners take away from the learning experience. Anticipating learner responses is also part of flexible and responsive teaching, which is further explored in Chapter 6.

Anticipating responses for every single open-ended task would be unsustainable. Rather than trying, focus on similar responses for different tasks that address similar skills. To begin, choose a couple of tasks for which you might anticipate responses over the course of an entire unit. You can do this alone, but the process is even richer when completed with colleagues.

Embed Assessment into the Learning Period

Embedding assessment into the learning period saves time and energy, reducing the amount of work teachers need to bring home. It also benefits students by providing high-quality feedback in the moment, shortening feedback loops and giving learners insight they can incorporate in reflection and planning action steps for the following day.

The descriptions of journal-based, portfolio, and verbal closing reflection above include some options for assessing within the learning period. Assessments might take place outside of class time, but this is not inherently bad—so long as you are not taking piles of paper home to grade. As you develop your assessment calendar, consider setting aside time in your schedule for reviewing student work on the days you administer formal assessments, perhaps even blocking out your entire planning or prep time.

You will not be able to assess during the learning period if you spend your time lecturing from the front of the room. Sage-on-the-stage teaching is unsustainable for many reasons; in the context of assessment, it is unsustainable because the time you spend in front of the class telling students things they will likely forget is time you could spend with small groups or individual students, engaging learners in feedback-laden conversations. Feedback should be related to a task students are currently working on, as opposed to a task or learning artifact from prior days. Short feedback loops are efficient, maximizing a teacher's time. When feedback loops are long, feedback becomes unactionable because too much has transpired in the interim.

I write feedback directly on learners' artifacts or affix sticky notes to them. When reviewing learners' portfolios, I can review previous feedback to keep them growing. Structures or rituals establish boundaries for how much feedback I give them, which benefits us both: I am able to conference with more kids, and they are not overloaded with feedback.

In the case of formal pre- and post-assessments and other formal assessment tasks, consider adding a reflection day to your calendar, preferably the day after the assessment is administered. This day will give students some time to process their strengths and errors and an opportunity to identify their next steps. If possible, set aside an entire learning period, because a lot of your time will be spent in one-on-one or small-group conversations. When learners finish reflecting, consider creating a learning menu that reviews and reinforces previous skills.

Limit Corrective Feedback

Teachers who overdo feedback are "going to reach a saturation point," shared Deanna Lough, a high school English teacher and instructional coach. Bringing up the example of a teacher who feels pressure to address every deficit in a student's writing, she stressed, "It's just not feasible to give *that* much feedback."

Bombarding learners with corrective feedback is unsustainable. First, this deficit-based approach is likely to chip away at intrinsic motivation. To build the resilience needed to work through productive struggle, kids need to feel a sense of mastery and competence—they need to feel like they are *good* at something. Limiting corrective feedback is one step you can take to create conditions in which learners feel empowered by your feedback. Too much corrective feedback will make them feel like they are drowning in their deficits. It is also just too much work for teachers. You will always encounter grammatical and spelling errors in writing, or see opportunities for learners to expand their thinking. But you cannot sustainably address all of a student's opportunities for growth within a short period of time.

Instead, identify one or two of the highest-impact opportunities for growth in their work. By clearly articulating success criteria in the beginning of a unit and using learner-friendly rubrics, you can direct learners to work on a specific skill or competency. For instance, in writing, I might disregard spelling temporarily to build elaboration skills. After identifying elaboration as a goal together with students, I would send them back to their tables to work on this goal, identifying a concrete time for follow-up, which may occur later in the learning period or the next day. Narrowing the scope of the feedback and limiting corrective feedback in the process make feedback sustainable for both learners and teachers.

Implications for Professional Learning

Learning is a process for kids, not a destination—and the same is true for educators. The process of growing as a teacher is messy. We take risks, we experience success, and we stumble upon moments of intense failure. But it is all a part of the process. Teachers develop an intuition for teaching—a keen mindfulness for what will and will not work—through trial and error. Professional learning should mirror that. Consider learning celebrations and learning labs as two process-oriented approaches to professional learning.

Learning Celebrations

Part of the work around sustainability, in both the classroom and in professional learning, entails identifying what lies within your control. Although there is a trend to decenter standardized assessments in our definitions of "success" in schools, such assessments are here for the foreseeable future. The need to analyze standardized test data and review the results as a school, on teams, or in individual classrooms is unlikely to change anytime soon.

This reality should not prevent educators from seeking additional ways to reflect on learner and teacher progress in schools. Creating other means by which to evaluate progress may very well drown out some of the anxiety and shame that inevitably accompany standardized metrics.

Learning celebrations provide an opportunity for school staff to come together around innovative practice; teachers receive validation for their successes and encouragement from thought partners as they reflect on changes they need to make to their practice. One structure for a learning celebration ritual uses similar prompts to the ones for students' verbal closing reflections:

- What worked this year?
- What didn't work?
- What's next?

These questions could be framed within a schoolwide goal, for example, if your school had set a goal around cultivating learner agency. But they can also remain open-ended if you are just starting to build your ritual.

Using a structure for reflection that mirrors what teachers and students use in the classroom creates parity between classroom and professional learning practice. Learning celebrations are most effective when grounded in evidence of student learning, so consider encouraging or even requiring educators to use student work or classroom videos as a means for reflection. Reflecting without direct references to tangible results will not be meaningful and will not contribute to the overall sustainability of engaging in the process of reflection. If teachers require scaffolding with this new way of thinking about professional learning, share a template using Google Docs or Google Slides and provide time during professional learning community (PLC) meetings to prepare for learning celebrations. The template should have space for teachers to record evidence of student learning in the form of work samples, and provide reflection prompts that ask teachers to articulate the effects specific practices had on learning artifacts. The practices analyzed could include ones that led to substantive student learning or observations of learning challenges that could be addressed in the future. You may even consider having teachers draw from student samples over the course of the year for PLC work, or invite coaches to facilitate this reflection process in PLCs.

Within the framework of backward design, a learning celebration serves as the evidence of learning in relation to the desired results. The yearly schoolwide goal (e.g., learner agency) is the desired result; the learning celebration provides an opportunity for reflection on a series of performance tasks (e.g., classroom practice, learning artifacts). Learning celebrations should be part of the big-picture planning for professional learning, linked to PLC work, and teachers should be aware of the timetable for events (e.g., end of each semester or term). These qualities make the ritual purposeful, relevant, and ultimately sustainable, as it is linked to and embedded in teachers' other core responsibilities. Most of all, it sets the tone for professional learning: *in this school, everyone is a learner—and that includes the teachers.*

Learning Labs

Too often, teachers attend professional learning outside of the school building. This can be a sign of deficit-based thinking: there are not enough gifts within the school to help teachers learn in community with each other.

It can also be very expensive to keep sending teachers elsewhere for professional learning. External professional development often claims a disproportionate amount of funding and energy when a lot of great things that can be amplified are already happening in schools.

Learning labs offer a solution that is both asset-based and more financially responsible. Consider the following learning lab process, influenced by my experience engaging in lesson study supported in part by the Chicago Lesson Study Alliance (www.lsalliance.org), headed by Tom McDougal and R. Akihiko Takahashi. The process consists of four steps: planning, teaching, debriefing, and follow-up.

Planning. About one month prior to the lesson, the host team (including available coaches and administrators) collaborates on planning the research lesson. In this meeting, the team crafts, revises, or clarifies a question that relates to the school's professional learning theme, if one exists.

Next, the host team forms a hypothesis for a research question. The team collaboratively creates a lesson plan for how to explore the research question, including choosing core materials for the lesson and contextualizing the lesson within a broader unit or sequence of lessons. Finally, the team generates ideas for assessment and documentation opportunities, including rubrics, checklists, and student work samples.

Teaching. The goal of the host lesson is to get an authentic view of what learning looks like in the host classroom; the guests are there to collect data. Although the presence of guests may modify student behavior and responses, the guests' goal is to act as flies on the wall—observers and not participants.

Guests might consider collecting data on all students using various methods; others might observe specific pods of students, taking note of student moves in relation to the research question. Guests should be encouraged to notice freely while keeping the research question and hypothesis in mind to frame their observations.

Debriefing. The learning lab should be debriefed using a formal structure as soon as possible, while participants' reflections are fresh in their minds (see Figure 5.5). Using a timer keeps the debriefing moving along.

Follow-up. Before the lab lesson debriefing concludes, participants should set a date and time for following up in one to two weeks. When teams follow up, preferably in partnership with a coach, they will reflect on action steps identified in the debrief. This practice both serves as a point of accountability and offers space for further reflection to determine the efficacy of the action steps. Follow-up ensures that the reflections from the learning lab have been put into action to ensure further student learning.

FIGURE 5.5

Debrief Discussion

Agenda Item	Duration
Host teacher provides initial comments, using the following prompts (Reins, 2020): • How did the lesson go compared to what was planned? • What did the teacher observe? • If the teacher deviated significantly from the plan, why, and what was the result? • Did new questions arise that the teacher would like to discuss?	5 minutes
Planning team members share observations and raise questions, using the host teacher prompts if helpful. During this time, the host teacher is not invited to respond to observations or questions.	5 minutes
Remaining guests share one observation or reflection using the following thinking stems: • I noticed . . . • I think . . . • I wonder . . .	2–3 minutes per person
Host teacher responds with final reflections, using the prompt: Based on personal reflections and comments, what steps do you want to take moving forward?	5 minutes
Participants complete a reflection, documenting key reflections, questions, and action steps to explore in future lab lessons.	10 minutes

Embracing the Process to Promote Flexibility

When teachers allow themselves to be vulnerable to varied learning processes, they create opportunities to be flexible with instruction. This flexibility is critical but also nuanced. Teachers can leverage anticipated learner responses and projected learning pathways to aid flexibility; they can also leverage their partnerships with learners to chart their own paths in the classroom. However, this level of flexibility is only possible through intentional planning and the use of a framework within which to assess student learning.

Unsustainability in the classroom is a result of not being able to harness the energy that comes from the consistent generation of evidence of learning. Flexible and responsive instruction can and should be the result of minimalist instruction design and draw from reflections on meaningful, process-driven evidence of learning.

Chapter Summary

The story of learning is what matters most in the classroom, and teachers can partner with learners in telling this story through process-driven assessment. This practice is sustainable because it mindfully decelerates learning, encouraging learners to self-reflect and gain insight into their own competency, increasing the likelihood that they will be able to make productive, educative choices with their burgeoning autonomy and share in the demands of sustaining learning. Most important, this story creates meaning, which allows learning to be sustained in the long term. Encouraging and allowing learners to make choices on their own means that teachers need to be flexible and responsive. This does not mean putting out fires all day long or bending until you break. Instead, it means anticipating learners' responses to tasks and creating a learning environment that can bend with them.

STOP AND REFLECT

Identify some action steps you can take to shift toward process-driven assessment.

- **Amplify:** Which sustainable practices are you already implementing that you want to keep or increase?
- **Alter:** What do you want to change or stop entirely?
- **Activate:** Which new practices would you like to implement to work toward sustainability?

6

Flexibility over Fixedness

ESSENTIAL QUESTION: How might learning be self-sustaining?

In Fall 2017, I began teaching 3rd grade at a new school. The 3rd grade team had previously had a less-than-flattering reputation at the school, although all of us were new to the team that year. It was unclear whether our "newness" was going to work in our favor or against us, but one thing I knew was that as a new team overcoming such a reputation, we were going to encounter our own sets of challenges.

We had heard that the previous team had difficulty with consistency between classrooms, so our team vision included boundaries related to consistency and autonomy. The previous team had taken varied approaches to curriculum and assessment practices, too, leading to significant differences in instructional approaches. Too much variation between classrooms within a given grade level can create unsustainable inequities; in some cases, this variation can even generate competition between teachers, chipping away at collectivist team practices.

  When teachers partner with each other, they share in the energy demands of sustaining learning across a grade level or even the entire school.

In response to the previous team's challenges, there was a push for my new team to operate with consistency. We were all experienced teachers, and there were many things that were worth collaborating on—common assessments for unit plans, parent communications, reflecting on evidence of student learning. These points of convergence are sustainable, allowing for partnership and camaraderie among teachers. Too much convergence, however, is inherently unsustainable. It engenders fixedness and rigidity, creating a codependency among teammates, with teachers relying too much on each other for basic planning and preparation.

Through camaraderie, teachers learn from each other and share the responsibility of long-term planning, creating short- and long-term rituals around guiding and reflecting on student learning. This in turn creates a cadence over the course of the school year as teachers engage in a cycle of planning units, assessing student learning, and reflecting on practice. Camaraderie is regenerative, too, allowing teachers to come together and recharge their batteries through connection and collaboration. If teaching is to be sustainable, teachers need to find support in the camaraderie of a teaching team while still feeling empowered by their own agency and professional knowledge. That said, each team will need to find the just-right balance of consistency and autonomy through trial and error.

Fixedness Is Unsustainable

An elementary instructional coach in Indiana described the "focus on assessments and data" as motivating school districts to find "the right magic curriculum solution and mandating that curriculum to fidelity." Complete fidelity across classrooms and grade levels is not possible, they noted, resulting in "teachers being minimized and devalued as those pushes continue."

> When teachers work together, opportunities arise for individuals to step up and step back, granting some the opportunity to recharge while others take the lead.

Fidelity came up frequently in responses to the #SustainableTeaching survey: curriculum committees or administrators decide to adopt a program or resource for everyone to use, a handful of trainings take place (or sometimes none at all), and teachers are expected to implement the curriculum with "fidelity." This term is often used euphemistically, its positive connotation hiding the implied meaning, which is that instructors must follow the curriculum exactly as written.

Too often, when teachers do not get the results district officials hope for, "fidelity" is identified as the issue: "Oh, well, you didn't implement the curriculum with fidelity. That's why it didn't work." Because the program officials have chosen appears to be backed by research, they assume that consistent implementation of the program on a broad scale, almost like an industrialized assembly line, will lead to the desired results. This unsustainable scenario ignores the messy, uncertain humanity of teachers and learners and overlooks the fact that curricula and other foundational resources are created by flawed human beings with biases colored by lived experiences. Due to the number of variables, it is virtually impossible to create a plug-and-play curriculum that can be implemented with "fidelity." This line of reasoning only sets teachers up for failure and further funnels funds to curriculum companies when the next new research-based manual comes out.

Framing the solution to low test scores as a fidelity issue makes achievement a "teacher problem," ignoring the many systemic constraints teachers are under and contributing to the systemic abuse of teachers in schools. Because fidelity is impossible, it sets up a dynamic that makes it easy for administrators and broader society to make teachers the scapegoat for the failures of the education system at large.

This reductive reasoning also fails to address the complexity of what teachers do in classrooms. They are not just deliverers of curriculum: they are confidants, friends, therapists, surrogate parents, snack providers, hug givers, and many other things. They see the humanity of their students and, as a result, know that a one-size-fits-all, seemingly faithful approach to packaged curriculum will not provide every learner with what they need in the classroom.

Flexible and responsive teaching, on the other hand, can add to the benefits of process-driven learning to enhance teaching sustainability. This approach makes learning a conversation—a cyclical exchange where energy is routinely exchanged between learners and teachers. In self-sustaining learning there is neither a beginning nor an end, just an exchange of ideas that lead to new learning over the course of a school year. Your willingness to be flexible and meet learners where they are makes it more likely that the learning will reach your students and make it into their long-term memories.

Finding Flexibility to Enhance Responsive Instruction

A choir teacher in Illinois described flexibility as putting "the student at the center of learning. This means taking a look at the data of the student learning level and [making] decisions on the learning in the classroom." This is the heart of responsive instruction. When teachers feel empowered to respond to learners' needs, learning becomes both equitable and emergent. Learners have access to what they need in the classroom to be successful while playing a critical role in a conversation that leads to meaningful, relevant, and sustained learning.

Equitable

Teachers who are flexible and responsive in their teaching create opportunities for equity. Achieving equity requires meeting the needs of all learners and having the evidence to show that learners' needs have, in fact, been met. Although teachers can anticipate responses from learners, they must also be prepared to meet unanticipated needs. This may require changing course in the moment—a failure to follow a curriculum with fidelity. What is more important than fidelity to a resource? Meeting all students' needs.

Equity entails much more than meeting students' academic needs; it means meeting their *human* needs first. Teachers must be able to adapt based on learner identity, as well as social, emotional, or cultural needs. Learners can be partners in the process of pursuing equity in the classroom. In fact, considering learner identity and creating conditions for learner empowerment invites students to think flexibly, making choices that help them meet their own needs and support others in getting what they need. This is a win-win for sustainability: learners reap the benefits of learning with independence, and teachers reap the benefits of sharing the emotional, physical, and spiritual demands of learning with students.

Achieving equity is an ongoing process. At any given moment within your classroom and school, someone's needs are *not* being met. When considering both sustainable and equitable practices, ask, "Who is currently left out? What needs to change to include those who have been inadvertently left out?" Teachers must have the agency to speak up, and administrators must be willing to listen.

A middle school English language arts teacher from Missouri shared, "I can't critique my school's equity practices because we're already better than other schools." But comparing one school's equity practices to those of other schools is itself inequitable. Different schools have different populations and, therefore, different needs. Equity work is not a competition—a notion that is itself inequitable, marginalizing some for the sake of hierarchy. To be both sustainable and equitable requires constantly seeking to improve equity practices and allowing all stakeholders to critique them.

Emergent

It is hard to determine where a field of grass originated, because rhizomes grow in networks with no identifiable source. Rhizomes come from other plants, producing offshoots from root systems. Over time, these root systems emerge and evolve into more sophisticated networks of roots. The roots and the plants grow in a tropistic fashion, moving toward external stimuli like sunlight, water, and temperature.

Learning can emerge and evolve in classrooms, too, under the right conditions and when we think of our classrooms as networks of learners. Gardeners spend time creating conditions for plants to thrive in their gardens and monitoring the overall health of the garden, responding by watering, pruning, or fertilizing. A teacher's job is to partner with learners to create the conditions necessary for fruitful learning to occur. Teachers should be spending the majority of their time tending to the overall health of their classroom, responding in the moment by supporting and enriching learning through feedback and task modifications.

In order for learning to emerge, learners and teachers alike must have agency to make decisions in the moment. They must see their identities as part of the collective consciousness of the classroom in order to contribute to it. They must feel emboldened by the *process* of learning to grapple with its uncertainty and continue growing. And, finally, they must know it is safe to take risks, make mistakes, and otherwise respond to the learning conversations that are happening all around them.

 Simple but effective learning rituals allow for learning to emerge on its own, in a shared responsibility between learners and teachers.

Classrooms require structure. Classrooms without structure can be chaotic and confusing for learners, leading to unproductive struggle and cognitive dissonance. Conversely, humanizing structures create mindful ritual, emotional safety, and the space to engage in rich learning conversations. With the proper structures and systems in place, teachers can trust that learning is emerging even when they are not there to witness it.

STOP AND REFLECT

- Are you, in your classroom or school, already teaching with flexibility and responsiveness?
- In what ways are your school or classroom equitable, allowing different types of learners' needs to be met?
- What steps have you taken to allow learning to emerge in your classroom?

Flexible Pedagogy Through Productive Structures and Tools

Flexibility presents a bit of a paradox. It does not mean letting kids do whatever they want in the classroom. Instead, it requires using productive structures and common tools that enhance a teacher's ability to respond to learners while providing options for learners to go down different paths (see Figure 6.1).

It is important to note that these tools or structures require that students be taught how to use them. For some students, open-ended tasks or a journaling-based curriculum may be a new experience. When building your classroom culture, consider that responsibility for new routines will need to be gradually released onto learners for them to experience success and independence.

Open-Ended Tasks

Open-ended tasks can encompass a broad swath of learning activities along a continuum. Any provocation, text, or task can run the continuum of open and closed, depending on how the task itself is set up. Cohen and Lotan (1997, 2014) define open-ended tasks as learning tasks that allow students to do the following:

- Grapple with uncertainty and ambiguity.
- Devise different plans, explore different paths, and generate multiple methods.

- Reach multiple solutions or no solution at all.
- Manage a dilemma.
- Solve an authentic problem.
- Become intellectual authorities on a topic.

A task does not need to meet all of these criteria, but teachers should create a rationale using at least some to consider a task open-ended.

Chapter 5 discussed anticipating student responses. Figure 5.4 illustrated how learners could use different plans or methods for showing ways to make 5s: they could draw pictures, write expressions, or use colored snap cubes or other manipulatives to demonstrate their methods. The variation of methods illustrates the flexibility of the task.

FIGURE 6.1

Structures and Tools for Flexibility

Structure or Tool	Description
Open-ended tasks	Universally designed with varied access points, these tasks are both minimalist and flexible, allowing learners to choose their own methods and draw different conclusions from a common activity.
Workshop model	A structure within which learners can converge and diverge, offering predictability while allowing teachers to respond to learners in small groups or one-on-one.
Journaling	A flexible tool for documenting the process of learning and letting learners explore their ideas, journaling structures provide students scaffolds for organizing content yet are open-ended enough that students can produce unique interpretations of a task or prompt.
Structured writing strategies	Reluctant and/or emerging writers often need strategies for elaboration and revision. Buckner's (2005) *Notebook Know-How* identifies a plethora of strategies to support learners, providing both structure and flexibility as they build independence in the writing process.
Thinking routines	Thinking routines (Ritchhart et al., 2011) provide both structure and flexibility with deepening thinking. These thinking routines can be used orally in whole-group, small-group, or conferencing settings; they can also be used as journaling structures.
Learning menus	Providing learners options for extended practice or enrichment in the classroom, menu items are intentionally chosen to address elements of deconstructed standards, including prerequisite skills, tasks for building fluency in grade-level skills, and enrichment.
Learning rituals	Rituals provide replicable and reliable structures within which learners can grapple with new content. The replicability of these learning rituals does not engender mindlessness or monotony; instead, they allow students to explore new content on their own, using a familiar routine to support them.
Arc-style planning	Teachers curate a selection of tasks related to broad learning goals over the course of a week or two. Based on learners' responses to tasks, teachers can change the order of tasks or add new tasks to the learning plan.

Flexibility also draws upon minimalism through universally designed tasks. Instead of creating different tasks for different groups of learners, a single universally designed task is intended to meet the needs of all learners by anticipating what different learners will need to grow within the task.

I created an open-ended task for students using *One Tin Soldier,* a 1969 antiwar song by Dennis Lambert and Brian Potter. The first two verses of the song tell the story of two groups: the mountain people and the people of the valley. The valley folk are vying for the buried treasure of the mountain people, who share their treasure with the people of the valley.

To make this task open-ended, I invited learners to write the third verse on their own, using the structure and syllabication of the first two stanzas as a support. This required them to use prediction skills, consider story structure, and identify the type of lesson the author (songwriter) might want readers or listeners to take away. The diversity of responses was humbling, creating rich conversations around learning while keeping learners focused on the concomitant learning objectives: prediction, story structure, and theme. Most of all, a task like this is self-sustaining—and, therefore, sustainable. Planning it is rather simple: anticipate learners' responses and consider how to facilitate a conversation that guides them toward deep understanding, using the workshop model, described below, as a flexible structure.

When teachers create open-ended tasks that are universally designed with varied access points, planning for instruction becomes simpler and more sustainable.

Workshop Model

When I was a new teacher, I used to plan lessons in a rigid, step-by-step manner. As any seasoned teacher knows, planning in rigid steps is unsustainable; it sets one up for almost certain failure. Lessons rarely go as anticipated, and teachers must be free to respond in the moment to learners. Moreover, planning too rigidly is simply not best for kids. For students to own their learning and truly be partners in the process, they must have the chance to spread their wings and make decisions.

The workshop model (originally developed by Lucy Calkins and Carmen Fariña) provides a sustainable solution, allowing for points of both convergence and divergence within a lesson structure. The notion of convergence and divergence within a lesson is sustainable because it allows for moments where teachers can work with their whole classroom full of students while

Flexible and responsive instruction is sustainable, in part, because it grants teachers opportunities to partner with learners and encourages learners to make decisions for themselves.

incorporating open-ended tasks. It is important that lesson structures have space for teachers to work with the entire class at times. As discussed in Chapter 4, it is not sustainable to fully individualize curriculum (despite the seductive marketing of personalized-learning companies). Finding points of convergence when the entire class can connect through universal learning tasks builds community, camaraderie, and a sense of belonging, proactively addressing issues of status and inequity (Cohen & Lotan, 1997). It also allows for a cyclical "catch and release" of students, allowing teachers to vary the lengths of independent and small-group learning time as students gradually build their agency.

The simplest structure for the workshop model consists of three sections: a minilesson, a workshop, and reflection. For the minilesson, the entire class comes together to engage in a common learning experience, which might entail the following:

- Making sense of a task learners will work on in small groups
- Modeling a reading or writing strategy
- Teaching a new game intended for fluency practice during independent and small-group work
- Reflecting on lessons from days prior

After the minilesson concludes, learners begin working in small groups or independently. During this time, learners might be working on the task shared in the minilesson and using journals to document their thinking. Or they could be applying the reading strategy from the minilesson to their independent reading books or engaging in the writing process. Meanwhile, the teacher has time to pull out groups or meet with learners one on one, embedding assessment and feedback into the learning period. This model is sustainable in part because it relies on partnership with learners. Learning is a shared responsibility, with learners able to make choices in their independent and small-group time.

The success of the workshop model is dependent upon learner agency, which is why it is important to shift your mindset toward collectivism and learner empowerment while also shifting toward flexibility. You must design activities that are regenerative in nature so that kids never feel like they are "done learning." They must know there is always something else they can do, even if it is as simple as reading independently and journaling about their reading. In a writing workshop, this can be as simple as starting a new piece when they feel they have finished a draft, revising writing using a learned strategy (editing for spelling, punctuation, or grammar), or seeking out a peer for feedback. In math, it could entail pulling out a math game or math project from a resource library in the classroom.

More sophisticated workshop models might have several points of convergence, including both a minilesson at the start of workshop and a mid-workshop minilesson where learners can reflect on what they have accomplished partway through the learning period. Mid-workshop minilessons allow teachers to "catch" learners and respond to their needs in the moment—eliminating the need to provide written feedback later (a sustainable practice). They are also sustainable because they are easy to plan: you can use anticipated responses, observations, and informal assessments from the first portion of the learning block to guide reflection. If there are no universal misconceptions or teaching points that need to be shared with the whole class at the midpoint, the minilesson can provide a time for learners to share work samples with the whole class to receive feedback and praise from peers. Sharing work samples provides learners with additional models of what journal responses, methods, or applications of the minilesson can look like, building agency over time. It may be appropriate to have multiple mid-workshop check-ins, scaffolding independence through the catch-and-release benefits that the workshop model offers.

> Regenerative activities are sustainable because teachers do not need to instruct students on next steps when the students feel they have finished.

This model is part of the effort to make learning a conversation in the classroom. The notion of learning as a conversation lies at the heart of responsive instruction. Responsive learning is a constant exchange of ideas that build upon one another and allow learning to emerge. The structures used to build lessons enable this type of responsive conversation, whether in the points of convergence, in conversations between students during the workshop, or in conversations teachers facilitate during small-group work and conferencing.

Again, in the workshop model, teachers rely on learners to operate with agency, which emphasizes the importance of creating conditions within which learners can harness their intrinsic power. Learners must feel empowered to operate with agency and make decisions that contribute to the flexibility of the learning environment. It is not enough to simply tell learners to operate with agency. Classrooms must be designed with flexibility in mind, providing students with tools and structures they can use on their own while explicitly teaching routines and gradually releasing these routines for them to exercise with independence.

Journaling

In my classrooms, journals are central to sustainability. They are minimalist (reducing my reliance on worksheets and excess busywork); they are process-oriented (less about the correct answer and instead placing emphasis on a learner's process); and they are flexible, their versatility conducive to all sorts of tasks. Journals also hold learners accountable for documenting their process over the course of a learning period. For open-ended tasks and the workshop model to be effective and the lessons learned transferable, learners must play an integral role in documenting their learning along the way. This requires supplying learners with structures so journaling is predictable.

I learned the following journaling structure from Meghan Smith, a PhD candidate at Stanford University:

- **My Idea:** Learners share their thinking about the assigned open-ended task, using numbers, equations, pictures, or words to show their approach.
- **My Thinking:** Learners write about their method; the teacher may provide sentence starters (e.g., first, next, then, finally) as a structure for describing steps.
- **New Learning:** The teacher starts with a universal statement, if they want learners to have the same takeaway from the task; as learners become better versed with "new learning" statements, they can generate the statement themselves. How targeted the learning statement is depends on teacher needs and learner readiness.
- **My Reflection:** Students write about a success, a challenge, or how their thinking has changed over the course of the learning period.

Journal checklists. For journaling to provide flexibility for learners, they must know how to use their journals appropriately. Strong classroom routines are an important support, but learners must also exercise strong executive function skills to use their journals to respond openly and tell the story of their learning journey. To scaffold students' use of journals, consider creating checklists for each type of journal they will use (see Figure 6.2). These checklists clarify expectations and create opportunities for learners to self-assess their journaling practice.

Journaling checklists are designed along the same lines as the self-assessment rubrics discussed in Chapter 4; they are not intended as a daily formal assessment. I often facilitate reflection on the journaling checklists as a class, using multiple entries as evidence for appropriate use of the journals. You will need to create separate rubrics for specific academic outcomes.

Although the sample checklists in Figure 6.2 are designed for elementary learners, the format can easily be adapted to meet the needs of older learners. Change the criteria to elicit the types of journals you want to see. Rubrics may also be adapted to meet the needs of learners who experience barriers to writing, including English learners or students with learning disabilities. You might consider making a modified rubric with expectations aligned to their needs, such as using voice-to-text or even video journals. You can also encourage English learners to journal in their home language.

Feelings journals. Learners need a place to process feelings. Sometimes this can be done with a trusted friend or adult, but often there is neither time nor space during class to process in the moment.

"I want to hear about the conflict you had at recess," I said to Heidi, one of my 3rd grade students, after lunch, "but we need to start our read-aloud. Will you go and write a feelings journal, and then I can talk with you about it when we transition to P.E.?"

Heidi nodded, returning to her seat for the start of the read-aloud, using the feelings journal structure I had previously introduced to the class:

- **My Feelings:** Students name their feelings using an "I feel..." statement.
- **My Story:** Students tell their side of the story.
- **My Next Steps:** Students share what they would like to do in response to the situation and their feelings.

Providing students with an opportunity to write in their feelings journals to process a conflict or challenge is a sustainable practice. Heidi had a place to put her feelings, giving her some space and time to de-escalate. I was able to continue my plans and provide the rest of the class the attention they needed after lunch. Heidi also received the validation and processing time she needed with me, after she had time to collect her thoughts and make some decisions about what she wanted to do with her feelings.

FIGURE 6.2

Sample Journaling Checklists

Math Journal Checklist	Not Yet	Starting To	Got It!
I wrote the date.	☐	☐	☐
I shared my idea using pictures, words, or numbers.	☐	☐	☐
I shared my thinking in words.	☐	☐	☐
I wrote a new learning statement.	☐	☐	☐
I included a reflection.	☐	☐	☐

Thinking Journal Checklist	Not Yet	Starting To	Got It!
I wrote the date and a title.	☐	☐	☐
My journal has a clear main idea.	☐	☐	☐
I used evidence to support my thinking (personal connections, text evidence).	☐	☐	☐
I incorporated my own experiences, personal connections, or questions to deepen my thinking.	☐	☐	☐
I included a reflection.	☐	☐	☐

Writing Journal Checklist	Not Yet	Starting To	Got It!
I turned to the next clear page and wrote the date and a title.	☐	☐	☐
I skipped lines to make space for revising and editing.	☐	☐	☐
I wrote legibly, inside the margins and on the lines.	☐	☐	☐
I used what I know about spelling to make my best attempt. I circled words I'm curious about.	☐	☐	☐

Structured Writing Strategies

Writing instruction often feels unsustainable because teachers carry too much of the cognitive and emotional load for learners. This is, in part, because educators embrace the industrialized and process-driven mindsets surrounding curriculum and pedagogy, convincing themselves that students will only be successful if their end products look like the exemplars.

My greatest hope for emerging writers is that they come to understand that their voice has value. Yes, they need to learn to structure their writing, but this does not necessitate teaching writing formulaically. It also does not require teachers to inch students toward replicating an exemplar. Instead, exemplars should serve as examples for what writing *can* look like (as opposed to what it *should* look like), and teaching should be geared toward helping writers think critically about their writing and how to employ strategies for different parts of the writing process. Two of my favorite writing strategies, Try Ten and Lift a Line, come from Aimee Buckner's (2005) *Notebook Know-How:*

- **Lift a Line** helps students with elaboration. When learners "lift a line," they select it from a page and rewrite it on a clean page. Then they describe and elaborate as much as they can, using sensory details or literary devices to expand on it.
- **Try Ten** is great for revising. Teachers create an unsustainable cycle of dependence when learners rely on them for identifying needed revisions. Sometimes, a sentence just does not sound quite right for a reason that is hard to pin down. Try Ten asks learners to rewrite a given line or sentence in 10 different ways, inviting them to get curious and play with language.

Strategies like these are sustainable because, first, they are minimalist in nature. Having a few of these strategies on hand for learners to access in the moment creates a ritual and a reliable structure that can be applied to all sorts of writing. These strategies are also sustainable because they empower learners to use them independently and engage in self-reflection, tapping into the empowerment mindset shift discussed in Chapter 3. Letting go of control and letting learners exercise these strategies on their own—even if it means their writing does not turn out like teachers might have hoped—is good for both students and teachers in the long run. It enables flexibility in the classroom, allowing learners to use strategies to better their writing as they see fit.

Thinking Routines

The goal of sustainable teaching is to help teachers shoulder more reasonable workloads while ensuring that students are learning in a sustainable way. For learning to be sustainable, it must be deep and transferable. Teaching solely for the efficient acquisition of facts and figures increases the likelihood that students will not retain what they have been taught, and thus is a waste of time. On the other hand, being flexible and responsive and seeking out opportunities for deep, transferable learning leads not only to sustainable teaching but also to sustained learning that is meaningful and relevant to learners.

Thinking routines (Ritchhart et al., 2011) allow for reliable structures within which learners can both deepen their understanding of a given topic and learn to articulate the nuances of their thinking—a far cry from worksheet-based learning. Deep thinking needs to be scaffolded for learners, and thinking routines do just that by providing a sustainable structure for complex thinking. See, Think, Wonder is one of Project Zero's (2022) most widely used thinking routines. It nurtures noticing, inferring, and inquiring in learners. For example, when examining a primary source such as a political cartoon, learners can identify concrete images they see in the cartoon, make inferences about what these images mean, and then ask questions to promote future noticing and inferring. Teachers can use sentence stems like the following to support learners:

- **I see . . .** that Uncle Sam is holding his nose in the cartoon.
- **I think . . .** this means that Uncle Sam does not like the immigrant that is at the "gate" to the United States.
- **I wonder . . .** why Uncle Sam didn't want the immigrant to come into the United States. Why was he being so mean?

Thinking routine strategies can be applied to different disciplines and content, making them both minimalist and flexible. Ideally, once students learn how to use the routines, they will be able to use them in journaling and classroom discussion in small groups—and perhaps even independently. You only need a handful of thinking routines to get started. Once you get comfortable with them, you can use them interchangeably and without much planning or preparation. An extensive toolbox of thinking routines from the Harvard Graduate School of Education's Project Zero is available at www.pz.harvard. edu/thinking-routines.

Learning Menus

Learning menus are another part of a minimalist approach to curriculum design, requiring teachers to move away from the industrialization of curriculum and instead allowing learning to be flexible to meet students' varied needs. Educators tend to think of "work" in school in an industrialized and cyclical fashion: teachers assign the work, kids complete the work, teachers score it, and then the cycle starts again.

This cycle is unsustainable for several reasons. The need to keep coming up with resources for learners to consume forces teachers to resort to worksheet- or workbook-based pedagogies (perhaps even leveraging resources from sites such as Teachers Pay Teachers that are inconsistent in quality and effectiveness). This conception of "work" also increases the number of learning artifacts that teachers must review and assess. Although teachers do not have to assess every worksheet they assign, if a learning artifact is not assessed in some way, what is its purpose? Is it meaningful learning, or is it busywork?

Providing students with menus of activities (see Chapter 5) they can undertake after completing a task can solve these two problems of unsustainability, while also building learner empowerment and allowing for students' varied levels of mastery. Learning menu activities are not chosen at random; they address multiple standards for grade-level goals and meet anticipated needs of learners within a specific classroom (see the "Learning Menu" section of the sample unit plan in Appendix A). By using backward design, deconstructing standards, and anticipating various levels of proficiency, you can have such activities ready to deploy when needed, enhancing your flexibility as a practitioner.

Learning menu activities can also be easily differentiated. Math activities can vary by size of numbers, relating to standards from various grade levels, as is denoted in Appendix A. For instance, if learners are instructed to play Addition Top-It with single-digit numbers but find it too easy, they can be given the option to use two- or three-digit numbers. Learners can also use three or four addends to address other standards and add complexity to a menu activity like Addition Top-It. As you choose menu activities, consider how these activities might be extended or scaffolded in the moment. Literacy menu activities are even simpler. Learners can engage in self-selected independent reading or additional writing on topics of choice. If journaling has been incorporated, learners can journal about their independent reading, using journaling structures to support them. Literacy center activities like word sorts can also serve as a flexible learning menu choice.

These kinds of activities are minimalist yet regenerative because they can be played repeatedly, without requiring teachers to generate more consumables or other content. They are also mutually beneficial for learners and teachers: learners build fluency, and teachers reap the benefits of less time spent on material preparation. These activities also promote self- and peer assessment. Your students naturally want to win the games, so they are incentivized to check the answers of their peers and naturally motivated to calculate accurately.

    Learning menu items should be regenerative, meaning that learners can self-assess and repeat the activity to continue building fluency. By partnering with learners to make choices, teachers reduce the amount of energy needed to sustain learning, and students feel empowered.

You do not have to micromanage your students' choices! You can partner with them to discuss which choices they will exercise after they have finished their open-ended task for the day, sharing in the energy demands of sustaining learning. Rest easy knowing that no matter what learners choose, all activity choices are either reinforcing or enriching a necessary skill.

In Stage 3 of the learning plan (see Appendix A), choices are gradually added to the menu each week. This adjustment is critical for sustainability and to properly scaffold learner independence. As your menu grows and the year moves along, you can add or remove choices, providing learners both more agency and more self-awareness about their own needs. In time, learners will make choices based on what they know they need to practice. This outcome, too, enhances sustainability, because you will have less to manage. After you have used learning menus for a unit, you can easily log them in your unit plans for reuse the following year.

To create learning menus that offer productive independent choices, you need a rich resource library that is well organized and universally designed for diverse groups of learners. Rich resource libraries can also help you respond to needs that arise in the moment, enhancing your instructional flexibility.

For reading instruction, this could be as simple as curating a rich classroom library (see Chapter 1). In the beginning of the year, learners might help organize and label the library, generating excitement and helping them gain familiarity with potential book choices, as well as strengthening their understanding of genre and alphabetization. You will need to implement some sort of system for checking out books, which will help you gain insight into the types of books each learner is choosing. Your resource library will also need to include different types of lined paper, as well as varied types of writing utensils (e.g., tri-writes, grippies, pens) and coloring tools. You might even want to have some spelling resources on hand that learners can use when they encounter a challenging word to spell. Math instruction requires a rich library of math manipulatives, easily visible and accessible to learners. You want students to spend their time thinking about what they need to be successful with a task, not wasting time wandering about the classroom, unsure how to find the necessary tools. It is important to remember that sustainability is not simply about doing less work; it entails building systems that will support you later. Curating a resource library will feel laborious and perhaps even tedious at first, but once it is well organized, it will play a pivotal role in sustaining learning over the course of the year.

> Rich and well-organized resource libraries simplify planning and preparation for flexible learning choices.

Learning Rituals

Students will operate with greater independence if you build routines and rituals in your classroom that help them learn on their own. The more these rituals sustain themselves through learner competency and execution, the more sustainable your classroom will be. Don't be afraid to explicitly teach these rituals and review them regularly with learners.

Acknowledging the importance of self-sustained learning rituals reinforces the importance of collectivist classroom cultures that create the conditions for learner empowerment. Classroom cultures where learners feel empowered to make choices engender space for flexibility in instruction, specifically with learners making choices on their own. However, to make productive choices that contribute to the sustainability of learning, learners must have a consistent structure and routines to follow so that they know what to do (see Figure 6.3). Similar to the learning menu and learner-friendly rubrics, these tools will scaffold learner independence if posted publicly, modeled, and referred to regularly.

FIGURE 6.3

Learning Rituals

Morning work	When arriving in the morning: ☐ Hang up your belongings. ☐ Greet your teacher. ☐ Put your take-home folder on your desk. ☐ Put your lunch in the lunch bin. ☐ Choose from the learning menu.
Book selection	To select new books: ☐ Empty your books from your book bin. ☐ Browse the books in the library. ☐ Select a book, reading a page and using the five-finger rule to see if it's just right. ☐ Choose up to three books. ☐ Ask yourself: Do I have a good variety?
Math workshop	When using your math journal: ☐ Write the date at the top of the next clean page in your journal. ☐ Tape the new math task on that page. ☐ Read the task, to yourself or with a buddy. ☐ Draw a visual model of the task or get started solving the problem.
Peer feedback	When providing feedback to a peer: ☐ Find a successful spot, sitting across from or next to your peer. ☐ Partner 1 shares their piece. ☐ Partner 2 provides two compliments and one suggestion for improvement (see the Two Stars and a Wish rubric). ☐ Repeat the process, switching roles. ☐ Both partners identify action steps based on the feedback.
Structured word inquiry	When exploring a new word, record in your journal: ☐ What does the word mean? ☐ How is the word built? ☐ What are its relatives? ☐ How does pronunciation change?

Note: For information on structured word inquiry, see Bowers & Bowers, 2008.

 After being gradually released to learners, learning rituals can sustain themselves as learners execute them with independence.

Once learning rituals are in place, students can use them at will. For instance, once learners know how to select new books, they do not need to wait for your permission to do so: they can use their free time during independent reading to choose books on their own. Similarly, once they have learned the process for exploring new words, they can explore them using the tools and structures you've shared with them and only reach out for help when necessary. Rituals can be applied to any activity you want students to execute independently. Once they know how to do these routines on their own, they no longer need you to facilitate the routine for them, allowing you to devote time to the tasks your students really need you for—providing feedback, supporting learners facing challenges relating to learning tasks, or facilitating small-group work for enhanced personalization.

Arc-Style Planning

To plan in arcs, consider how lessons or tasks address different aspects of a learning goal, acting as building blocks toward a deeper understanding. Learning is not linear, and there are often multiple routes to the same learning goal, depending on learner readiness and how lessons transpire in the classroom.

In Arc 2 of the sample unit plan (Appendix A), students explore the properties of addition and subtraction. This arc consists of a projected sequence of activities, all related to the same learning goal. If you post learning targets on the board in your classroom, the tasks themselves can be associated with bite-sized learning objectives. For example, the Tyrone's Flowers task (described in Figure 5.4), which involves learners combining two colors of flowers into unique bouquets of five, lends itself to making 5s; the learning objective for students is "I can identify ways to make 5 with two addends." The More Flowers task (the next building block) increases the difficulty by asking learners to identify ways to make 10 and 20 with two addends.

The second task might require more time than you have in a single instructional period. Arc-style planning does not specify a timetable, empowering teachers to extend the task into another learning period so that learners have enough time to thoroughly document their methods, though I do recommend setting approximate goals for completing arcs to keep on track with yearly curriculum maps. If the More Flowers task proves difficult for a number of learners, you might spend more time the next day reinforcing making 5s, 10s, or 20s using one of the additional activities. (The sample unit plan in Appendix A also uses What's Behind My Back? as a formal assessment.)

Depending on the results of instruction, supported by process-driven assessment that asks learners to reflect on tasks daily, you may decide to change the instructional sequence, adding or omitting tasks as needed. This flexibility and responsiveness has the benefit of being sustainable, requiring little energy to make alterations once students already have rituals in place for journaling and encountering open-ended tasks. This is what makes arc-style planning sustainable: it provides you with a project task sequence that can be modified as needed, with all of the tasks supporting the broader learning goal and inching learners toward the end-of-arc formal assessment task.

Implications for Professional Learning

As mentioned in preceding chapters, there must be alignment between shifting the classroom teaching mindset and shifting the professional learning mindset. Encouraging teachers to be flexible with their teaching means that responses to their professional learning also has to be flexible. Professional learning communities (PLCs) offer a sustainable solution for flexible professional learning.

Teachers as Activators

In *PLC+: Better Decisions and Greater Impact by Design,* Fisher and colleagues (2020) build on DuFour and colleagues' (2010) four-question framework for PLC work, inviting teachers, coaches, and school leaders to consider five questions instead of four:

1. Where are we going?
2. Where are we now?
3. How do we move learning forward?
4. What did we learn today?
5. Who benefited and who did not?

Fisher and colleagues describe teachers as *activators* of PLC work, which strengthens the shift toward teacher agency. PLC time is used to learn about learning, as opposed to passively reviewing standardized test data or participating in a book club—which they call "PLC myths" (pp. 1–3). Although reviewing data and reading new research on teaching can support the PLC process—answering questions 2 and 3, respectively—these activities are insufficient if they do not relate directly to problems of practice within the classroom and are not grounded in reflection on evidence of student learning.

I recently used these five questions to partner with a school to create a student work analysis protocol (SWAP). The primary goal of establishing the SWAP was to unite the entire teaching staff in a common process for student work analysis, making it possible for teams to partner to analyze student samples vertically; such a schoolwide routine is ritualistic in nature.

Once the SWAP process is internalized, the cognitive load shifts toward the mindful analysis of student work, meaning the process is flexible and regenerative—and therefore sustainable. All teachers need to do is bring student work samples from the week and engage in the process. Although SWAP is perhaps most fruitful when teachers from different classrooms review common formal assessment tasks, it is still effective with informal samples from one teacher's classroom. Because the process is flexible and forgiving, it is sustainable. Furthermore, this process builds a skillset in teachers that influences conversations about learning outside of PLC. Teachers begin to analyze student work using more precise and action-oriented language, leading to richer conversations and enhanced self-reflection on teaching practice.

> Creating rituals around student work analysis leads to responsive, sustainable teaching grounded in evidence of student learning, thus providing an energy source for future learning.

Originally, I guided teachers through the five questions in relation to student work analysis. We eventually consolidated the five PLC+ questions into three major steps: orient, analyze, and consolidate. Figure 6.4 illustrates using

FIGURE 6.4

Student Work Analysis Protocol

Step	Prompts
1. Orient Where are we going? Where are we now?	Identify the learning goal or standard related to the artifacts you've chosen for today's analysis. Describe how the learning artifact fits into the learning plan.
2. Analyze How do we move learning forward? Who benefited and who did not?	*Think, Puzzle, Explore* What do these learning artifacts make you think? What are you puzzled by? What new evidence-based practices might you suggest or try?
3. Consolidate What did we learn today?	Reflect on new learnings: • I used to think _____. Now I think . . . • I used to _____. Now I will . . . • I realized . . . • Tomorrow/next week, I will . . .

Note: The *Think, Puzzle, Explore* thinking routine was developed by Project Zero (2019), a research center at the Harvard Graduate School of Education.

the five questions within these steps as both a structure and standing agenda for PLC meetings about student work analysis.

The process structure is flexible, which both keeps teams on track and creates space for them to surface insights about students and their learning. The thinking routines and structures also allow for flexibility, as they simply provide the language to get conversation flowing. The thinking routine may not be necessary if the conversation is rich and actionable. However, some teachers may not be accustomed to reflecting in this way. In those cases, the thinking routine scaffolds the conversation to get teachers talking deeply and actionably about student learning. As a SWAP facilitator, I always encourage educators to leverage their observations and reflections on these conversations to determine how much structure their team needs.

From Fidelity to Flexibility

If teachers are to be activators of professional learning (Fisher et al., 2020), they must regularly have access to evidence of student learning. SWAPs can support this data collection, but there also must be an explicit expectation that insights gained from generating evidence of student learning will directly result in action. This cannot happen without a flexible mindset around learning and the curriculum. In fact, some teams elect to add a "planning and preparation" step to the SWAP process, going into unit plans or creating additional resources to address action steps if time permits.

In the #SustainableTeaching survey, many teachers advocated for school districts to provide foundational resources so that teachers are not creating everything from scratch. One 3rd grade teacher in Illinois described relying on teachers to create a curriculum from scratch as "very unsustainable, [and] using Teachers Pay Teachers to produce an entire curriculum is very unsustainable, especially when using resources that are not culturally relevant to the makeup of [their] classrooms."

This sentiment gives a rationale for providing foundational resources from which teachers can curate learning experiences—but without coaches and administrators becoming the "fidelity police," a situation that sets everyone up for failure. A sustainable alternative is to recommend that teachers draw upon these resources and incorporate them into the backward design process (see Chapter 4 and Appendix A) so that teachers are constantly reflecting on evidence of student learning while leveraging sustainable foundational resources. These resources will aid teachers in making flexible and responsive instructional decisions that are grounded directly in learning artifacts resulting from executing the learning plan. "Fidelity" to a packaged curriculum will not result in rich, deep, and sustained student learning. Flexibility, responsiveness, and a solid learning plan, however, will.

Sustainable Teaching Leads to Sustained Learning

Teacher well-being is just as important as fruitful student learning. In sustainable classrooms, practices that benefit teachers also benefit students. Flexible teachers are liberated from the anxiety that comes from pressuring themselves into curriculum coverage, allowing them to create equitable learning spaces where learning can emerge and grow. This flexibility leads to deep and meaningful learning that sustains itself because it *sticks*.

When learning doesn't stick, you must have the courage to ask yourself, *Why isn't it sticking? What is the effect of this in the long term? And—most important—what are we going to change so that it does?* How can you use your new understanding of sustainability to make these changes?

Chapter Summary

For learning to be self-sustaining, it must be a conversation—an exchange of ideas between teachers and learners. Teachers must feel empowered to be flexible and responsive to learners to freely engage in conversations around learning. This allows learning to emerge, much like a healthy garden emerges with the mindful oversight of a gardener, responding to the needs of the garden as they arise. It also allows for learning to be sustained long-term, as learners' involvement in such conversations adds meaning and relevance. Assuming the proper conditions are set for independent and interdependent learning, teachers can tend to their classrooms like they would a garden, ensuring the conditions are ripe for growth. Being flexible means using structures in the classroom that support learners and scaffold learning, such as the workshop model, learning rituals, and learning menus.

STOP AND REFLECT

Identify some action steps you can take to shift toward responsive instruction.

- **Amplify:** Which sustainable practices are you already implementing that you want to keep or increase?
- **Alter:** What do you want to change or stop entirely?
- **Activate:** Which new practices would you like to implement to work toward sustainability?

Conclusion:
A Marathon, Not a Sprint

The journey toward sustainability must begin with an acknowledgment that we are, in fact, in a crisis. This assessment is not intended to incite panic but to help us come to terms with what it will require to address the current state of our profession. We must not only listen to teachers who take the brave step of voicing concerns but also *believe* them when they share that they are burning out.

In February 2023, during the final stages of editing this book, I came across this tweet from Nicole LePera (@Theholisticpsyc), psychologist and *New York Times* bestselling author:

> Maybe it's not burnout. Maybe it's a sign you're unappreciated and doing work that doesn't provide you with a sense of meaning or purpose. Maybe it's your body saying: no more of this.

While teachers should be paid more, we must remember that teaching is a profession of passion. By and large, people become teachers because they genuinely *want* to do this work. Stripping their agency, dignity, and integrity from them causes them to disengage. Why would anyone stay in a profession that underpays them, underappreciates them, deprives them of autonomy, and is devoid of meaning? No one would, if they could help it.

Addressing education's climate crisis starts here: with believing teachers, appreciating them, trusting them to be autonomous in their classrooms, and giving them the freedom to find purpose in their classrooms. I won't ignore the self-evident fact that teachers are grossly underpaid, and that long-term sustainability will only come with long-term investments in teachers. While we can keep fighting for equitable pay for teachers, this is often not a problem that teachers can solve on their own.

We can, however, take steps toward increased sustainability in our classrooms and schools—and all of us play a role in making teaching sustainable. We simply have to find that which is within each of our respective loci of control, set goals, and make tangible steps toward these goals in community with others. It is important to remember that the journey toward sustainability should itself be sustainable. Attempting to change everything overnight will not only lead more quickly to burnout but also generate feelings of hopelessness. What matters most in this journey is not that you cross any sort of arbitrary sustainability "finish line," but rather that you engage in the process of identifying unsustainable practices and setting goals to make them more sustainable.

Jim Knight's (2018) *The Impact Cycle* provides a foundation for this regenerative and self-sustaining process. By gaining a clear picture of the current reality in your classroom or school, you can identify which practices feel least sustainable. Use the mindset shifts discussed in the preceding chapters to identify new practices to explore. Consider how the six themes for sustainable teaching—healing, regeneration, vulnerability, ritual, simplicity, and partnership—apply to your current practice, and identify new practices that embrace these themes. Finally, set goals to improve sustainability in your classroom or school related to these new practices. This will bring you back to the beginning of the cycle: examining the effect these new, more sustainable practices have on your classroom.

If you are a practicing classroom teacher, this process will require embracing vulnerability. It's a courageous act to commit to change, especially when long-held practices and beliefs seem so safe and comfortable. If you are a coach or administrator, this will require creating supportive conditions in which teachers feel empowered and trusted to make the changes they believe will make their jobs more sustainable. Regardless of your role, a focus on partnership and healing is necessary. The past few years have been traumatic, to say the least—the climax of decades of educator oppression. We cannot solve every problem, but we can heal by connecting with one another through the collective purpose of improving working conditions in schools.

Sustainable practices not only help teachers preserve precious energy at school, they also produce sustained *learning*. Unsustainable practices lead to shallow learning experiences grounded in industrialized, rote memorization for the purpose of test performance. This learning (if we can even call it that) is ephemeral and quickly erodes, unable to transfer past the date of a high-stakes assessment—proving that it was never sustainable to begin with. It is exhaust, entropic in nature and dissipating into the abyss. Here is a litmus test: if working conditions and teaching practices allow teachers to regenerate their energy reserves while leading to transferable, deep learning for students, they are likely sustainable.

The suggestions in this book are simply a place to start. Given your knowledge of your students, your curriculum, and the barriers you face in your school or district, decide which entry point feels most accessible and will lead to the broadest and most sustainable impact.

To reach sustainability in teaching, we must create supportive conditions in which teachers have agency over their goals and goal setting. Administrators and coaches should act as sounding boards when teachers are setting goals and must support and trust teachers' assessments of the sustainability of their own practice.

Appendix B includes a goal-setting template to help you get started. The template prompts you to reflect on your current practices and how they align with the mindset shifts and themes of sustainability discussed in this book, and then to identify your strengths and challenges. Consider beginning with practices that are most within reach. If you are engaging in an excess of unsustainable practices, you may want to rank them by highest level of urgency or broadest influence. Once you've identified a goal to work toward, use the SMART framework (goals that are specific, measurable, action-oriented or attainable, relevant, and time-bound) to define it so you can put it into action. I encourage you to deeply explore how you might implement a new practice or incorporate improvements, and identify specific action steps that will help you lift the practice off the ground. The following guidelines for goal setting may help:

- To measure the efficacy of a practice, consider teacher energy and the capacity for the practice to lead to deep, sustained learning. Both qualitative and quantitative metrics might be appropriate for measuring success.
- Your goal should lead to tangible evidence of sustainability—reflections from teachers as well as evidence of student learning. This evidence will demonstrate that the practice is leading to meaningful learning experiences.

- Give yourself grace and space to explore the practice, reflecting every 8 to 12 weeks (coinciding with your terms or semesters). Then decide whether to continue working on this practice or shift your energies elsewhere, creating a new sustainability goal.
- Create a plan for progress monitoring with your team, instructional coach, or administrator. If reflections become part of your team or staff meetings, all stakeholders know they will be held accountable for reflecting on their goals regularly.

The cycle of setting sustainable goals and then reflecting on and adjusting them (or moving forward) is ultimately about creating professional learning rituals in which teachers can identify incremental shifts in practice that will eventually result in sustained, long-term shifts in practice. (It may also reveal that the implementation of a goal did not lead to increased sustainability in the short term.) Trust that adhering to this process will ensure that cycles of inquiry and reflection remain constant throughout the school year.

Shifting toward sustainability is a marathon, not a sprint. Attempting to change all aspects of practice overnight is not sustainable and is likely to result in frustration and negative effects on student learning. Teachers, coaches, and administrators alike must make the collective decision to commit to sustainability, using the six mindset shifts and accompanying practices as a inspiration for courageous and critical discussions.

Although it is true that education's core purpose is to serve learners and families, fulfilling that purpose is impossible if teachers are burning out and leaving the profession at increasing rates. Teachers will be more likely to stay in the classroom if their jobs are sustainable and they are treated with the dignity and respect they so deserve.

Personal sustainability looks different for each teacher, which is why it's paramount that we not only amplify teachers' voices in the process, giving them control over their sustainability goals, but also *believe* teachers when they identify practices as unsustainable.

Sustainability is a serious matter—and an existential one. We cannot afford to go back to the status quo, and we cannot trudge forward into a "new normal" that is just as unsustainable as our last version of normal. Addressing education's climate crisis is not a hopeless endeavor. The incremental shifts in practice that come from the exploration of sustainability may feel like small ripples at first, but with time and collective efforts, these ripples can create a #SustainableTeaching movement in your school and beyond. I look forward to hearing about and seeing the fruits of your labor.

Acknowledgments

There were hundreds of respondents to the #SustainableTeaching survey—teachers at all levels of education, administrators, special education teachers, special-area teachers, and counselors. Of these, I interviewed over 70 educators. Many preferred to remain anonymous; those mentioned in the text include the following:

Maribel (Mari) Gonzalez, STEM integration transformation coach, Technology Access Foundation, Seattle, WA

Lisa Julian Keniry, founder, Green Teach for Opportunity Project, Washington, DC

Destiny Lane, 3rd grade teacher, Louisville, KY

Leah Leonard, principal, Lexington, NC

Deanna Lough, English teacher and instructional coach, Georgetown, DE

Ricky Martin, instructional coach, Lexington, NC

Deanna Rice, science teacher, Toledo, OH

Friedrika (Fritzi) Robinson, elementary school teacher, Providence, RI

Paula Smeltekop, elementary teacher and media specialist, Glenview, IL

Allysun Sokolowski, elementary and middle school teacher, Bethesda, MD

Cassie Stokes, Portland Elementary School, Louisville, KY

Megan Sturgeon, Portland Elementary School, Louisville, KY

I am also grateful to Meghan Smith, PhD candidate, Stanford University, who introduced me to the use of a T-chart in developing rubrics and the journaling structure I use and describe in this book.

While many respondents wished to remain anonymous, I'd like to recognize those who have consented to be acknowledged for their contributions to the survey. Thank you for working with me to #MakeTeachingSustainable!

Nishat Alikhan

Emily Alt

Cara Bandalos

A'Lana Bates

Michelle Blais

Christine Bogart

Barbara Bray

Brittany

Ben Bruhn

Maggie Bryant

Geoffrey Carlisle

Connor Carson

Korleen Cosgrove

Erika De La Rosa

Linda Diekman

Barrie Fitzgerald

Steve Flores

David Frangiosa

Mariusz Galczynski

Eric Gold

Allyssa Graham

Edie Gray

Cuyote Corey Harkins

Kyle Harris

Emily Hart

Erin Healey

Laura Henderson

Danielle Kay

Dylan Kendall

Katie Kinder

Alison Koutroulias

Elizabeth Lerner

Jennifer Lucchino

Tessa Maguire

Wilmarie Maldonado
   Castro

Christal Manders

Kessler McClanahan

Finn Menzies

Adrienne Michetti

Megan Mkrtschjan

Lesley Moffat

Greg Moffitt

Robert Montgomery

Wendi Moss

Jillian Nettels

Jillian Peterson

Tony Quan

Matthew Rhoads, EdD

Katie Jo Robinson

Devin Rohr

Abby Sada

Michael Sivert

Dan Slagter

Laura Smolcha

Kanako Suwa

Jackie Tan

Jean Taraba

Alex Tougas

Rayanna Tremblay

Shelley S. Wagner, MA

Mandy Warren

Hayley Weeden

Rose Wehrenberg

Katie Weingarten

Hannah Wilson

Nicole Woulfe

Melanie M. Wright

I would also like to express my gratitude to all of the people who've supported me, not only in this project but also as I've transitioned into a career as a writer, coach, and consultant in education. Dan Alpert and Jim Knight were some of the first to take a chance on me and my writing. If not for them believing in me and giving me a chance, I would not be writing this book on #SustainableTeaching. I want to thank Carol Ann Tomlinson, an inspiring voice and mentor who has both encouraged and advocated for me. Her assistance in connecting with ASCD led to this publication.

I also want to thank the people who helped this book come to life. Allison Scott encouraged me to pursue the idea of #SustainableTeaching after a number of exploratory conversations. She helped me shape it into a pitch to ASCD, and her supportive words lit a fire under me. Genny Ostertag, my acquisitions editor, was an incredible thought partner as we shaped this book. Her insights transformed the manuscript into its current form, preserving the urgency of the message while offering hope and actionability to educators. I want to also acknowledge the contributions of Jennifer Morgan, who spent ample time with me and my indecision, as we contemplated and recontemplated titles, artwork, and subtle changes to the text to make this work as engaging and well articulated as possible.

Appendix A: Sample Backward Design Unit Plan

The following unit plan is adapted from instructional design work with multiple teachers from Portland Elementary School in Louisville, Kentucky, including Destiny Lane, Cassie Stokes, and Megan Sturgeon. *Illustrative Mathematics* (Kendall Hunt) and *Everyday Mathematics* (McGraw-Hill) are foundational resources. Language for the grade-level goals is from the *Common Core State Standards for Mathematics* (National Governors Association Center for Best Practices & Council of Chief State School Officers, 2010).

Stage 1: Desired Results

Established Goals	Transfer	
Represent and solve problems involving addition and subtraction. Use addition and subtraction within 100 to solve one- and two-step word problems involving situations of adding to, taking from, putting together, taking apart, and comparing, with unknowns in all positions, e.g., by using drawings and equations with a symbol for the unknown number to represent the problem.	*Efficiency* means taking the fewest number of steps to the end goal.	
	Meaning	
	Understandings	**Essential Question**
	Learners will understand that there is not a single method that is most efficient in math. The method used depends on the problem and the learner.	*What is most efficient?*
	Acquisition	
	Declarative Knowledge	**Procedural Knowledge and Skills**
Add and subtract within 20. Fluently add and subtract within 20 using mental strategies. Know from memory all sums of two one-digit numbers.	*Key Vocabulary* • **Efficient** • Addition (putting together, adding to, compare) • Subtraction (take away, taking apart, compare) • Solve • Equations • Symbol (plus, minus, equal) • Situation • Unknown • **Represent** • Solve • Sum • Difference • Graph (picture graph, bar graph, title, data/information, categories, scale) • Data	In order to **journal,** students will be able to: • Make a model to represent the task • Move left to right and top to bottom in the journal • Use the full space in the journal strategically • Organize their work logically • Choose tools that work for them such as concrete manipulatives (e.g., 10-frames, snap cubes, red/yellow chips), drawings, etc. • Record their use of a tool in their journal by drawing a picture or writing about it • Explain why they used a tool • Write legibly using the grids and lines • Self-evaluate their work compared with a model or other student's method • Write in their journal page by page
Represent and interpret data. Draw a picture graph and a bar graph (with single-unit scale) to represent a data set with up to four categories. Solve simple put-together, take-apart, and compare problems using information presented in a bar graph.	*Journaling/Agency* Students will be able to: • Identify parts of a journal • Identify strategies for what to do when they get stuck or feel frustrated • Identify feelings associated with failure or obstacles • Process instructions using rehearsal	In order to operate with **agency** in mathematics, students will be able to: • Communicate with peers about mathematics • Organize and find materials • Ask questions • Ask for help when appropriate • Choose a math game based on strengths and needs in math
Use place value understanding and properties of operations to add and subtract. Count within 1,000; skip-count by 5s, 10s, and 100s. Fluently add and subtract within 100 using strategies based on place value, properties of operations, and/or the relationship between addition and subtraction.	*Math Content* Students will know that: • Data are a type of information Students will be able to: • Identify parts of a picture or bar graph • Recount all of the ways to make 5 • Recount all of the ways to make 10	With regard to math content, students will be able to: • Read different types of bar or picture graphs • Construct a bar and/or picture graph to represent data collected • Use manipulatives to add and subtract within 20 and 100 • Decompose two-digit numbers into 10s and 1s • Decompose numbers less than 10 into 5s and 1s • Choose efficient strategies for adding and subtracting • Count on from a number • Represent an addition or subtraction situation using a bar model

Stage 2: Collecting Evidence

Evaluation Criteria	Performance Tasks
• I can solve word problems using adding and subtracting. • I can efficiently add and subtract within 20. • I can draw a picture or bar graph to represent data. • I can skip-count by 5s, 10s, and 100s up to 1,000. • I can efficiently add and subtract within 100.	• Unit 1 pre-assessment • Unit 1 post-assessment • Interview-based fact fluency and skip-counting • Formative assessment: drawing bar graphs • Formative assessment: adding and subtracting within 100
	Other Evidence
	Journals, selected exit slips

Stage 3: Learning Plan

Lesson Structure

All lessons will use a complex-instruction workshop model, involving moments of convergence and divergence.

Minilesson (10 minutes)	In the minilesson, teacher and learners make sense of the task as a group. Learners will read the task (either as a group or independently) and discuss the task by turning and talking to neighbors. Teacher and students may brainstorm potential strategies to solve the problem. Learners will be released when they feel like they know how to start the task in their journals.
Workshop (20 minutes)	Learners will work on their own or in small groups, grappling with each open-ended task and documenting their thinking in their journals. During this time, learners will do one of the following: • Finish the open-ended task (either independently or with partners/groups), using the existing journaling structure (My Ideas, My Thinking, My Reflection, New Learning). Students who finish the task early may engage in one of the learning menu choices (i.e., math game or enrichment project). All students have access to all activities and choices. *or* • Be pulled into small groups for intervention, supervised work, or teacher-guided facilitation of the open-ended task.
Discussion (15 minutes)	The mid-workshop discussion functions as a second minilesson. Learners will share methods and strategies for approaching the open-ended task. The goals of the discussion are the following: • Give learners agency through sharing their approaches. • Illustrate diversity of methods, building choice into open-ended tasks. • Instill a collectivist mindset in learners, demonstrating that learners of all ability levels can contribute to math discussion. • Build interpersonal communication skills around academic competencies.
Workshop (15–20 minutes)	During this time, learners will consolidate insights from the mid-workshop discussion, applying learned methods or new strategies to journaling. Learners may try another learner's method in their journal, demonstrating greater efficiency with regard to the open-ended task. Learners who realize they made a mistake in the process of solving the task may use a second method that corrects their error. Learners who decide that their math journal is complete may engage in one of the learning menu choices (i.e., math games or enrichment project).
Final reflection (10 minutes)	During this time, learners will complete the reflection portion of the journal. (Some students may have done this during the preceding workshop.) Next, the class will reflect together, and learners will do one or more of the following: • Share what they've already written in their reflections with a peer. • Write their reflection with the group, using a sentence starter (e.g., "I realized . . ."; "I used to . . . ; next time I will . . ."; "Tomorrow I will try . . ."; "[Another student]'s method made me think . . ."). • Reflect orally with a partner, using the sentence starters or open-ended reflections.

Journaling and Portfolios

All documentation will be housed in math journals and portfolios. This unit assumes that all learners have been introduced to these routines and can journal incorporating the four sections listed. Teachers will provide scaffolds for learners who are not yet able to journal with independence. All formal assessments will be collected in portfolios and paired with formal reflections (My Strengths, My Challenges, My Next Steps).

Process	Each day, learners will use their journals in concert with the workshop model structure. This journaling structure will consist of the following four components: • My Ideas • My Thinking • My Reflections • What I Learned

Learning Menu

The learning menu offers learners activities as after-task choices. Potential addressed standards are noted under descriptions of each activity, providing clarity into how tasks can be adapted to meet varying readiness of learners.

What's Behind My Back? (*Illustrative Mathematics*)	Learners work to decompose numbers into two addends. To differentiate the game, encourage learners to choose among 5, 10, and 20. One learner decomposes a set of snap cubes into two parts, hiding one of the parts behind their back. The other learner guesses what is hidden behind their back. Standards addressed: K.OA.A.3, K.OA.A.4, K.OA.A.5, 1.OA.B.3, 2.OA.B.2
Number grid puzzles	Learners can choose from a group of baggies containing 100s charts that are cut up into puzzle pieces. Using what they know about counting patterns and adding and subtracting 10s, partners or teams put the puzzle together. Standards addressed: 2.NBT.A.1, 2.NBT.B.8
Counting collections (Franke et al., 2018)	The counting collections resource library will have different collections of items. Learners will be encouraged to count them in various ways, leveraging their agency and naturally differentiating for ability level. Teachers may consider suggesting that learners count by a given number on a given week. Standards addressed: 1.NBT.A.1, 2.NBT.A.2, 2.OA.C.4
Race to 100	This game can be played in multiple variations, in a group, or by an individual. Learners may use a place-value chart or a 100s chart. Learners roll a die (6-, 10-, or 12-sided, depending on rigor level). With the 100s chart, they move that number of spaces. With the place-value chart, learners gather the number of unit cubes that correlate with their roll. Learners should be encouraged to add efficiently, moving beyond counting by 1s to add. Standards addressed: K.CC.A.1, 1.OA.C.5, 1.NBT.B.2, 2.OA.A.1, 2.OA.B.2, 2.NBT.A.1, 2.NBT.B.5, 2.NBT.B.8
Addition Top-It (*Everyday Mathematics*)	Learners use digit cards to add single-digit numbers. Each learner pulls two digit cards and announces the sum. The learner who has the higher sum wins the cards. This game can be adapted by inviting learners to choose the size and number of the addends (e.g., learners play with a two-digit and one-digit number, learners play with multiple addends). Standards addressed: 1.OA.B.3, 1.OA.C.5, 1.NBT.B.3, 1.NBT.C.4, 1.NBT.C.5, 1.NBT.C.6, 2.OA.A.1, 2.OA.B.2, 2.NBT.B.5, 2.NBT.B.6, 2.NBT.B.7, 2.NBT.B.8, 2.NBT.B.9
Subtraction Top-It (*Everyday Mathematics*)	Learners use digit cards to subtract single-digit numbers. Each learner pulls two digit cards and announces the difference. The learner who has the higher difference wins the cards. This game can be adapted by inviting learners to choose the size of the subtrahend and minuend (e.g., learners play with a two-digit and one-digit number, learners play with two multidigit numbers). Standards addressed: 1.OA.B.3, 1.OA.B.4, 1.NBT.B.3, 1.NBT.C.5, 1.NBT.C.6, 2.OA.A.1, 2.OA.B.2, 2.NBT.B.5, 2.NBT.B.7, 2.NBT.B.8, 2.NBT.B.9
Data collection	In this enrichment project, available to all students, learners collect data on a topic of their choice and make a bar or picture graph. Learners use grid paper in their math journals to draw lines and fill in boxes. Provide picture and bar graph templates to learners as needed. Standards addressed: 2.MD.D.10

Arc 1: Counting Collections (3–5 days)	
Introduce counting collections by providing each group with the same number of objects, teaching learners how to document their counting strategy in their math journal. Repeat the process of counting collections each day with varied numbers of objects. Consider choosing a day where learners have different amounts of objects.	
Learning goal	Students will learn how to use math journals and build routines for math workshop by engaging with counting collections. By the end of this arc, learners will know how to represent their math ideas in a math journal and write a sentence about their counting strategy.
Projected sequence	Lesson 1: Counting collection (24 snap cubes) Lesson 2: Counting collection (36 counting bears) Lesson 3: Counting collection (75 two-color counters)
Learning menu items	What's Behind My Back? (5, 10, or 20 cubes total) Number grid puzzles
Formal assessment	Learners complete a counting collection independently. They will draw their counting strategy in their math journal and write at least one sentence about their counting strategy.

Arc 2: Properties of Addition and Subtraction (7–10 days)	
Within each task, learners will show their ideas using pictures, words, or numbers; they will also write a sentence to explain their method. Learners will write a new learning and reflection statement.	
Learning goal	Learners will identify ways to compose and decompose numbers, learning that addition and subtraction can be represented by a variety of situations, including joining, separating, parts-and-wholes, and comparing.
Projected sequence	Lesson 1: Tyrone's Flowers task Lesson 2: More Flowers task Lesson 3: Joining situations Lesson 4: Separating situations Lesson 5: Part-part-whole situations Lesson 6: Comparing situations Lesson 7: Represent visuals using different equations
Learning menu items	What's Behind My Back? (5, 10, or 20 cubes total) Number grid puzzles Independent counting collections
Formal assessment	Learners will complete a teacher-presented What's Behind My Back? using 17 cubes total.

Arc 3: Adding and Subtracting Within 20 (4–6 days)	
Teachers will discuss efficient strategies for adding and subtracting, specifically 10-frames, base-10 blocks, number grids, open number lines, and decomposing numbers to make 10s. Encourage students to move from concrete strategies (e.g., 10-frames, base-10 blocks) to abstract strategies (e.g., composing and decomposing numbers to make 10s).	
Learning goal	Learners will build fluency adding and subtracting within 20, using counting collections and their knowledge of different situations to support them.
Projected sequence (*Illustrative Mathematics*)	Lesson 1: Add and subtract within 10 Lesson 2: Related addition and subtraction within 10 Lesson 3: Related addition and subtraction within 20 Lesson 4: Add and subtract your way
Learning menu items	Race to 100 Addition Top-It (within 20) Subtraction Top-It Number grid puzzles Independent counting collections What's Behind My Back? (5, 10, or 20 cubes total)
Formal assessment	Learners will engage in a mid-unit interview-based fact fluency assessment. Teachers will look for increased sophistication of mental strategies.

Arc 4: Data and Measurement (9–11 days) *Teachers will explicitly link data collection and representation to computation skills. Addition and subtraction tasks will build fluency on previously taught strategies, while the focus of lessons will be on data collection and representation.*	
Learning goal	Learners will apply addition and subtraction skills within 20 to read, interpret, and make calculations using bar graphs. Students will use grid paper to construct their own bar graphs.
Projected sequence	Lesson 1: Collect and represent data Lesson 2: Interpret picture graphs Lesson 3: Interpret bar graphs Lesson 4: Represent data using picture graphs and bar graphs Lesson 5: Questions about data Lesson 6: Use bar graphs to compare Lesson 7: Use diagrams to compare Lesson 8: Diagrams with all kinds of compare problems Lesson 9: Solve all kinds of compare problems
Learning menu items	Data collection project Race to 100 Addition Top-It (within 20) Subtraction Top-It Number grid puzzles Independent counting collections What's Behind My Back? (5, 10, or 20 cubes total)
Formal assessment	Learners will read a graph of different ways students get to school and answer questions about the graph: Which is the most common way to get to school? Which is the least common? How many students were surveyed in total? How many more students took the bus than a car?

Arc 5: Adding and Subtracting Within 100 (5–7 days) *Students will extend addition and subtraction skills from previous arcs, applying them to adding and subtracting within 100. Teachers will focus on concrete, representational, and place value strategies to build number sense and dexterity with computation. Students may use the standard algorithm but will be directed to demonstrate understanding using multiple algorithms.*	
Learning goal	Learners will add and subtract within 100, using a variety of strategies, including decomposing numbers, open number lines, number discs, base-10 blocks, and other derived mental strategies.
Projected sequence	Lesson 1: Add Within 50 task (*Illustrative Mathematics*) Lesson 2: Pencils and Stickers task (*Illustrative Mathematics*) Lesson 3: Doggy Day Care task Lesson 4: Dog Food task Lesson 5: You Won a Prize! task
Learning menu items	Data collection project Race to 100 Addition Top-It (within 100) Subtraction Top-It (within 100) Number grid patterns Independent counting collections What's Behind My Back? (5, 10, or 20 cubes total)
Formal assessment	Learners will complete the Paul's Lawn-Mowing Business task: Paul has a lawn-mowing business. This table shows how much money he made each day over the course of one week.

DAY	AMOUNT
Sunday	$ 5.00
Monday	$17.00
Tuesday	$ 4.00
Wednesday	$13.00
Thursday	$ 6.00
Friday	$18.00
Saturday	$25.00

1. How much money did Paul make in total?
2. Choose two days to compare. How much more did he make on one day than the other?

Appendix B: Goal-Setting Template

The start of your journey with #SustainableTeaching should be intentional and action oriented. Use this Goal-Setting Template to reflect on what you've learned through each of the six mindset shifts, identifying your strengths and challenges with sustainability in Step 1. For Step 2, use the SMART framework to identify a sustainability goal; this can be done schoolwide, in teams, or even individually. Once you have set your goal, be sure to outline a clear action plan in Step 3.

Step 1: Identify Strengths and Challenges		
Use your reflections from Chapters 1–6 to identify your strengths and challenges related to sustainability. Collaborate as needed with colleagues, coaches, and administrators to ensure you have the clearest picture of your current reality.	Strengths	Challenges

Step 2: Goal Setting		
Choose one of your challenges for goal setting.	To which of the mindset shifts does this apply? ☐ Humanity over industry ☐ Collectivism over individualism ☐ Empowerment over control ☐ Minimalism over maximalism ☐ Process over product ☐ Flexibility over fixedness	Which sustainability themes are lacking in this unsustainable practice? ☐ Healing ☐ Regeneration ☐ Vulnerability ☐ Ritual ☐ Simplicity ☐ Partnership
	Further describe how the unsustainable practice relates to these mindset shifts or themes:	
Use the SMART framework to identify a specific goal that is measurable, action-oriented or attainable, relevant, and time-bound.	**What is your goal?** Make sure your goal is specific, articulating clear shifts in culture, practice, or resources with actionable and observable steps. **How will you measure progress toward your goal?** Identify qualitative and quantitative indicators for success. **How do you know your goal is achievable?** Explain how you know this goal is a sustainable goal to set for yourself this year. (Remember, you don't have to solve every problem!) **In what ways is your goal relevant?** Discuss how your goal supports district or school initiatives or solves a major problem of practice in the classroom. Share how you hope achieving this goal will change your classroom or school. **When do you hope to achieve this goal?** Discuss a timeline to monitor progress toward your goal, and identify a time for a summative evaluation.	

Step 3: Action Plan		

Describe concrete action steps you will take. Consider identifying deadlines for each action step and assigning them to team members if you're working on a team (see example).

Action Step	Deadline	Owner
Create learner-friendly rubric for Unit 1 of math.	*August 15*	*Paul*

References

Almarode, J., Hattie, J., Fisher, D., & Frey, N. (2021). *Reinvesting and rebounding: Where the evidence points for accelerating learning.* Corwin Press.

Belsky, G. (n.d.). *The 3 areas of executive function.* Understood. https://www.understood.org/en/articles/types-of-executive-function-skills

Bowers, S., & Bowers, P. (2008). *Understanding SWI: "Structured word inquiry" or "scientific word investigation."* WordWorks Literacy Centre. https://wordworkskingston.com/WordWorks/Structured_Word_Inquiry.html

Brackett, M. (2019). *Permission to feel: Unlocking the power of emotions to help our kids, ourselves, and our society thrive* (1st ed.). Celadon Books.

Brackett, M., & Cipriano, C. (2020, April 7). *Teachers are anxious and overwhelmed. They need SEL now more than ever.* EdSurge. https://www.edsurge.com/news/2020-04-07-teachers-are-anxious-and-overwhelmed-they-need-sel-now-more-than-ever

Brown, B. (2010). *The gifts of imperfection: Let go of who you think you're supposed to be and embrace who you are.* Hazelden.

Brown, B. (2017). *Braving the wilderness: The quest for true belonging and the courage to stand alone.* Random House.

Buckner, A. (2005). *Notebook know-how: Strategies for the writer's notebook.* Stenhouse.

Burns, E., & Frangiosa, D. (2021). *Going gradeless, grades 6–12: Shifting the focus to student learning.* Corwin.

Campbell, D. T. (1979). Assessing the impact of planned social change. *Evaluation and Program Planning, 2*(1), 67–90. https://doi.org/10.1016/0149-7189(79)90048-X

Carver-Thomas, D., & Darling-Hammond, L. (2017). *Teacher turnover: Why it matters and what we can do about it.* Learning Policy Institute. https://learningpolicyinstitute.org/sites/default/files/product-files/Teacher_Turnover_REPORT.pdf

CAST. (2018). *The UDL guidelines.* https://udlguidelines.cast.org

Cohen, E. G., & Lotan, R. A. (1997). *Working for equity in heterogeneous classrooms: Sociological theory in practice.* Teachers College Press.

Cohen E., & Lotan, R. (2014). *Designing groupwork: Strategies for the heterogeneous classroom* (3rd ed.). Teachers College Press.

Crenshaw, K. (1989). Demarginalizing the intersection of race and sex: A Black feminist critique of antidiscrimination doctrine, feminist theory and antiracist politics. *University of Chicago Legal Forum, 1989*(1), article 8. https://chicagounbound.uchicago.edu/uclf/vol1989/iss1/8

Croft, S. J., Roberts, M. A., & Stenhouse, V. L. (2015). The perfect storm of education reform: High-stakes testing and teacher evaluation. *Social Justice, 42*(1), 70–92. https://www.socialjusticejournal.org/archive/139_42_1/139_05_Croft_Roberts_Stenhouse.pdf

Danielson, C. (2009). *Implementing the Framework for Teaching in enhancing professional practice.* ASCD.

Darwich, L., & Thompson, A. (2021, November 10). *A sustainability strategy for new teachers.* Edutopia. https://www.edutopia.org/article/sustainability-strategy-new-teachers

Del Carmen Unda, M., & Lizárraga-Dueñas, L. (2021). The Testing Industrial Complex: Texas and beyond. *Texas Education Review, 9*(2), 31–42. https://doi.org/10.26153/tsw/13911

DeWitt, P. (2022). *De-implementation: Creating the space to focus on what works.* Corwin.

Dietz, M. (2000, July). *Single-point rubric idea.* Presented at INTASC Academy, Alverno College, Milwaukee, WI.

DuFour, R., DuFour, R., Eaker, R., & Many, T. (2010). *Learning by doing* (2nd ed.). Solution Tree.

Dweck, C. S. (2008). *Mindset.* Ballantine Books.

Emdin, C. (2016). *For white folks who teach in the hood . . . And the rest of y'all too: Reality pedagogy and urban education.* Beacon Press.

Ernst-Slavit, G., & Egbert, J. (n.d.). Chapter 5: Connecting to students' lives. In *Planning meaningful instruction for ELLs.* https://opentext.wsu.edu/planning-meaningful-instruction-for-ells/chapter/chapter-5/

Fahy, J. K. (2014). Language and executive function: Self-talk for self-regulation. *Perspectives of the ASHA Special Interest Groups, 21*(2), 61–71.

Farber, K. (2010). *Why great teachers quit: And how we might stop the exodus.* Corwin Press.

Fisher, D., Frey, N., Almarode, J., Flories, K., & Nagel, D. (2020). *PLC+: Better decisions and greater impact by design.* Corwin.

France, P. E. (2019). One vision, many paths. *The Learning Professional: The Learning Forward Journal, 40*(4). https://learningforward.org/journal/personalizing-learning/one-vision-many-paths/

France, P. E. (2020). *Humanizing distance learning: Centering equity and humanity in times of crisis.* Corwin.

France, P. E. (2022). *Reclaiming personalized learning: A pedagogy for restoring equity and humanity in our classrooms* (2nd ed.). Corwin.

France, P. E., & Almarode, J. (2022). Learning to notice. *Educational Leadership, 80*(3), 26–32. https://www.ascd.org/el/articles/learning-to-notice

Franke, M. L., Kazemi, E., & Chan Turrou, A. (Eds.). (2018). *Choral counting & counting collections: Transforming the preK–5 math classroom.* Stenhouse.

Garcia Winner, M. (2002). *Thinking about you, thinking about me.* Social Thinking.

Garcia Winner, M. (2008). *Think social! A social-thinking curriculum for school-age students.* Think Social Publishing.

Hammond, Z. (2015). *Culturally responsive teaching and the brain: Promoting authentic engagement and rigor among culturally and linguistically diverse students.* Corwin.

Hastings, M., & Agrawal, S. (2015, January 9). *Lack of teacher engagement linked to 2.3 million missed workdays.* Gallup. https://news.gallup.com/poll/180455/lack-teacher-engagement-linked-million-missed-workdays.aspx

Herek, S. (Director). (1995). *Mr. Holland's opus* [Film]. Hollywood Pictures.

HMH & YouGov. (2021). *7th annual educator confidence report.* https://www.hmhco.com/documents/educator-confidence-report-2021

Houghton Mifflin Harcourt & YouGov. (2020). *2020 educator confidence report.* https://www.hmhco.com/documents/educator-confidence-report-2020

Jacobsen, K., & Ward, S. (2016). *Strategies for improving executive function skills to plan, organize, and problem solve for school success.* https://www.glenbardgps.org/wp-content/uploads/2016/06/sarah-ward-executive-function-lecture-handout-December-6-2016-Glenbard-IL.pdf

Johns, M. M., Lowry, R., Haderxhanaj, L. T., Rasberry, C. N., Robin, L., Scales, L., Stone, D., & Suarez, N. A. (2020). Trends in violence victimization and suicide risk by sexual identity among high school students—Youth Risk Behavior Survey, United States, 2015–2019. *Morbidity and Mortality Weekly Report Supplement, 69*(1), 19–27. https://www.cdc.gov/mmwr/volumes/69/su/su6901a3.htm

Jotkoff, E. (2022, February 1). *NEA survey: Massive staff shortages in schools leading to educator burnout; alarming number of educators indicating they plan to leave profession* [Press release]. NEA. https://www.nea.org/about-nea/media-center/press-releases/nea-survey-massive-staff-shortages-schools-leading-educator

Keene, E. O., & Zimmermann, S. (1997). *Mosaic of thought: Teaching comprehension in a reader's workshop.* Heinemann.

Knight, J. (2018). *The impact cycle: What instructional coaches should do to foster powerful improvements in teaching.* Corwin.

Kuypers, L. M. (2011). *Zones of regulation: A curriculum designed to foster self-regulation and emotional control.* Social Thinking Publishing.

LaGravenese, R. (2007). *Freedom writers* [Film]. MTV Films.

Lambert, D., & Potter, B. (1969). One tin soldier [Song recorded by The Original Caste]. On *One Tin Soldier.* Bell.

Madrigal, S., & Garcia Winner, M. (2009). *Superflex takes on Glassman and the Team of Unthinkables.* Think Social Publishing.

Marzano, R. J. (2009). *Formative assessment & standards-based grading* (Ill. ed.). Marzano Research Laboratory.

Moeller, J., Ivcevic, Z., White, A. E., Menges, J. I., & Brackett, M. A. (2018). Highly engaged but burned out: Intra-individual profiles in the US workforce. *Career Development International, 23*(1), 86–105. https://doi.org/10.1108/CDI-12-2016-0215

Moll, L. C., Amanti, C., Neff, D., & Gonzalez, N. (1992). Funds of knowledge for teaching: Using a qualitative approach to connect homes and classrooms. *Theory into Practice, 31*(2), 132–141. https://doi.org/10.1080/00405849209543534

National Center for Education Statistics. (2021). Characteristics of public school teachers. *Condition of Education.* U.S. Department of Education, Institute of Education Sciences. https://nces.ed.gov/programs/coe/indicator/clr

National Commission on Excellence in Education. (1983). *A nation at risk: The imperative for educational reform.* U.S. Department of Education.

National Governors Association Center for Best Practices & Council of Chief State School Officers. (2010). *Common Core State Standards for mathematics.* https://learning.ccsso.org/common-core-state-standards-initiative

Okun, T. (2022). *White supremacy culture* [Website]. https://www.whitesupremacyculture.info

Paris, D. (2012). Culturally sustaining pedagogy: A needed change in stance, terminology, and practice. *Educational Researcher, 41*(3), 93–97. https://doi.org/10.3102/0013189X12441244

Paris, D., & Alim, H. S. (2017). *Culturally sustaining pedagogies: Teaching and learning for justice in a changing world.* Teachers College Press.

Pink, D. (2009). *Drive: The surprising truth about what motivates us.* Riverhead Books.

Project Zero. (2019). *Think, puzzle, explore. A thinking routine that sets the stage for deeper inquiry.* Harvard Graduate School of Education. https://pz.harvard.edu/sites/default/files/Think%20 Puzzle%20Explore_3.pdf

Project Zero. (2022). *See, think, wonder.* Harvard Graduate School of Education. http://www. pz.harvard.edu/sites/default/files/See%20Think%20Wonder_3.pdf

Puentedura, R. R. (2015). *SAMR: A brief introduction.* http://hippasus.com/rrpweblog/ archives/2015/10/SAMR_AbriefIntro.pdf

Reich, J. (2022). The power of doing less in schools. *Educational Leadership, 80*(2). https://www. ascd.org/el/articles/the-power-of-doing-less-in-schools

Reins, K. J. (2020). Designing effective lesson study practices for mathematics education students. *Educational Designer, 4*(13). http://www.educationaldesigner.org/ed/volume4/issue13/article52/

Responsive Classroom. (2015). *The first six weeks of school.* Center for Responsive Schools.

Responsive Classroom. (2016, June 7). *What is Morning Meeting?* https://www.responsiveclassroom. org/what-is-morning-meeting/

Ritchhart, R., Church, M., & Morrison, K. (2011). *Making thinking visible: How to promote engagement, understanding, and independence for all learners.* Jossey-Bass.

Thompson, D. (2022, August 24). There is no national teacher shortage: The narrative doesn't match the numbers. *The Atlantic.* https://www.theatlantic.com/newsletters/archive/2022/08/ national-teacher-shortage-turnover-student-enrollment/671214/

Tomlinson, C. A. (1999). *The differentiated classroom: Responding to the needs of all learners.* ASCD.

Valenzuela, A. (1999). *Subtractive schooling: U.S.–Mexican youth and the politics of caring.* State University of New York Press.

Walqui, A., & Van Lier, L. (2010). *Scaffolding the academic success of adolescent English language learners: A pedagogy of promise.* WestEd.

Wiggins, G., & McTighe, J. (2005). *Understanding by design* (2nd ed.). ASCD.

World Population Review. (n.d.). *Common Core states 2023.* https://worldpopulationreview.com/ state-rankings/common-core-states

Zamarro, G., Camp, A., Fuchsman, D., and McGee, J. B. (2021, September 8). *How the pandemic has changed teachers' commitment to remaining in the classroom.* Brookings. https://www.brookings. edu/blog/brown-center-chalkboard/2021/09/08/how-the-pandemic-has-changed-teachers- commitment-to-remaining-in-the-classroom/

Index

The letter *f* following a page locator denotes a figure.

About the Author

Paul Emerich France is a National Board Certified Teacher, literacy specialist, keynote speaker, and author of two previous books, *Reclaiming Personalized Learning* and *Humanizing Distance Learning*. In his writing and speaking, he aims to convey one central message: we must teach and learn in the pursuit of a deeper sense of collective humanity—and for no other reason. Paul's work with #SustainableTeaching also stems from this principle: to make teaching sustainable, we need to first and foremost value the humanity of teachers and create conditions in which they can thrive.

Paul has contributed to a number of online and print education-related publications, including Edutopia, EdSurge, ASCD's *Educational Leadership,* the International Literacy Association's *Literacy Today,* and Learning Forward's *The Learning Professional.* His work has been featured at SXSW EDU and in *The New Yorker, WIRED,* and *The Atlantic.*

Paul currently consults with teachers, schools, and school districts and offers educational support to families in pods and one-on-one settings. You can learn more about him and his work by following him on Twitter (@SustainTeaching) and visiting his website (https://maketeachingsustainable .org).

Become a Sustainable School

Visit https://maketeachingsustainable.org to learn more about becoming a sustainable school. The site offers tools to help you conduct a sustainability audit, ways to partner with Paul for administrative and instructional coaching, and a link to the *Make Teaching Sustainable* podcast.

Related ASCD Resources: Sustainable Teaching

At the time of publication, the following resources were available (ASCD stock numbers in parentheses):

The Burnout Cure: Learning to Love Teaching Again by Chase Mielke (#119004)

Creating a Culture of Reflective Practice: Capacity-Building for Schoolwide Success by Pete Hall and Alisa Simeral (#117006)

Educator Bandwidth: How to Reclaim Your Energy, Passion, and Time by Jane A. G. Kise and Ann Holm (#122019)

Making Teachers Better, Not Bitter: Balancing Evaluation, Supervision, and Reflection for Professional Growth by Tony Frontier and Paul Mielke (#116002)

Manage Your Time or Time Will Manage You: Strategies That Work from an Educator Who's Been There by PJ Caposey (#119005)

The Minimalist Teacher by Tamera Musiowsky-Borneman and C. Y. Arnold (#121058)

Overcoming Educator Burnout (Quick Reference Guide) by Chase Mielke (#QRG123016)

Teach Happier This School Year: 40 Weeks of Inspiration and Reflection by Suzanne Dailey (#123027)

Teach, Reflect, Learn: Building Your Capacity for Success in the Classroom by Pete Hall and Alisa Simeral (#115040)

The Well-Balanced Teacher: How to Work Smarter and Stay Sane Inside the Classroom and Out by Mike Anderson (#111004)

For up-to-date information about ASCD resources, go to www.ascd.org. You can search the complete archives of *Educational Leadership* at www.ascd.org/el. To contact us, send an email to member@ascd.org or call 1-800-933-2723 or 703-578-9600.

WHOLE CHILD
TENETS

1 **HEALTHY**
Each student enters school healthy and learns about and practices a healthy lifestyle.

2 **SAFE**
Each student learns in an environment that is physically and emotionally safe for students and adults.

3 **ENGAGED**
Each student is actively engaged in learning and is connected to the school and broader community.

4 **SUPPORTED**
Each student has access to personalized learning and is supported by qualified, caring adults.

5 **CHALLENGED**
Each student is challenged academically and prepared for success in college or further study and for employment and participation in a global environment.

ascd whole child

The ASCD Whole Child approach is an effort to transition from a focus on narrowly defined academic achievement to one that promotes the long-term development and success of all children. Through this approach, ASCD supports educators, families, community members, and policymakers as they move from a vision about educating the whole child to sustainable, collaborative actions.

Make Teaching Sustainable relates to the **safe** and **supported** tenets. *For more about the ASCD Whole Child approach, visit* **www.ascd.org/wholechild.**